Esker beroenak eman nahi dizkiet Juan Jose Belza Artieda, Marcos Balentziaga Larrañaga eta Rupert Odorika Ezkurdia Adiskide eta lankideei, itzulpen hau aurrera ermaten eskaini didaten laguntza baliosaren gatik.

M. Dean Johnson

An Audio Program

Especially created to accompany this book are 4 instructional audio cds or 2 audio cassettes. They are available from the publisher.

Learning Basque (Euskara Ikasteko Metodoa)

Copyright ©1995 Xabier Gereño
All rights reserved.

No part of this publication may be reproduced, stored in a retrieval system, or transmitted, in any form or by any means, electronic, mechanical, photocopying, recording, or otherwise, without the prior written permission by the publisher.

ISBN 1-57970-166-3 Text and Cds
0-88432-874-0 Text and Cassettes
0-88432-875-9 Text

This edition published by AudioForum,
One Orchard Park Road, Madison, CT 06443 USA
www.audioforum.com

Printed in the United States of America.

EUSKARA IKASTEKO METODOA

LEARNING BASQUE

Xabier Gereño

FOREWORD

The Unified Basque, or Euskara Batua, presented in this book represents a decade of work and research undertaken as a labor of love by many Basque linguists and historians. Because of the adverse political and economic conditions under which this endeavor has been carried out, the emergence of publications in Batua may be seen as a very real achievement for two reasons.

The unification of Basque has had the important consequence of helping the language to transcend dialect boundaries, thus permitting verbal and literary communication to exist and flourish throughout Euskalherria on all subjects—from poetry to nuclear physics. And the very existence of Batua is indicative of, and in some measure responsible for, the resurgence of a language which came close to extinction under the repression of the last forty years.

The opportunity to learn Basque is therefore both a hard-won privilege and a way of contributing to the permanent existence of this ancient language whose extinction would represent an irreparable loss. One of the aims of this book, then, is to enable students from other countries to share in the resurgence of Basque culture through the acquisition of a language which has become symbolic of a heroic people's struggle for survival.

Madison, Connecticut

TRANSLATOR'S PREFACE

The study of a new language is always a double adventure. The student is not only examining new linguistic (and therefore psychological) structures or patterns of thought, but he or she is also, of necessity, examining his or her own language in a new light. The student is contrasting the syntactic structures or thought processes which were always taken for granted as "logical" in the native language with new, and often very different, linguistic patterns. When there is a close equivalence in structures between the two languages, the student has relatively few problems. But when the structures are very different, or when subtle shades of meaning cannot be translated, difficulties inevitably arise.

In studying the Basque language, the English-speaking student will soon become aware of three major areas of difficulty. The use of the definite and indefinite articles in Basque does not correspond to English usage; the auxiliary verbs, besides having numerous conjugations, express in their morphological structure certain relationships which the English speaker does not need to analyze in English. The prepositions, which play a vital role in both English and Basque, and which in Basque are added to their (declinable) objects in the form of suffixes, rarely correspond to just one English equivalent, but can be translated in various ways. Anyone who has tried to explain to a foreigner the subtle difference between "jumping off a wall" and "jumping from a wall," or being "at someone's house" as opposed to being "in someone's house," will realize just how difficult it is to teach or translate these differences without loss of meaning.

In translating this book, certain difficulties have arisen due to its very structure. In its original form, the book was intended for students whose native language is Spanish, and the brief grammatical explanations and notes given in each lesson therefore explained only those aspects of Basque which might cause difficulty for Spaniards. The student was then expected to learn the structure under discussion by analyzing numerous sentences designed to illustrate it.

Both the explanations and the examples, however, are often inadequate for the English-speaking student. Brief translator's notes have therefore been provided wherever space permitted their insertion, and two translations of the examples have often been given, the second appearing in parentheses. This second, more literal, translation has been provided for the first few examples of a similar type whenever new structures are being introduced in order to help in analysis. Parentheses may also indicate that some words have been added to the translation in order to help in analyzing the Basque, or to render the sentence fully intelligible in English.

Since Basque does not distinguish between masculine and feminine in the third person singular, the pronoun "he" has generally been used throughout. The second person, "you," has both a singular and a plural form in each conjugation, but this difference is pointed out only in the first few lessons.

Because this method is intended for the general public rather than for linguists, I have tried to keep grammatical terminology to a minimum. Giving necessarily brief grammatical explanations in lay terms has perhaps been the most difficult task of all in translating this book. Nevertheless, both the author and I share the hope that through conscientious analysis of the examples, the student will be able to overcome the difficulties that arise and come to enjoy the very real adventure that learning Basque is.

M. Dean Johnson

Introduction

This method has been designed for people who wish to learn the Basque language without the help of a teacher. In order to take maximum advantage of this method, the learner must bear in mind the following recommendations:

1. First observe the structure of the book:
   a) In Part One, there are 40 lessons of identical extension and distribution.

   b) Part Two of the book is made up of complete charts of conjugations and declensions. This second part can be consulted as a guide when doubts arise, or in order to achieve greater perfection in the use of the verbe at a more advanced stage of learning. The charts, however, are not indispensable, since the most common verbal forms contained therein are introduced in the 40 preceding lessons.

2. This book uses a basic vocabulary of approximately 1,000 words.

3. Some 1,300 sentences are included, along with their translations.

4. The translations have been provided in order to make it possible for the learner to use the dictionary as little as possible.

5. The greatest difficulty for the learner of Basque resides in the verb. The learner must therefore dedicate as much time and attention as possible to this aspect of the language.

6. WE EARNESTLY RECOMMEND that the sentences contained in each lesson be learned by heart. By doing so, the learner will be simultaneously:

   a) learning vocabulary
   b) learning how to construct sentences
   c) mastering the use of the verb
   d) acquiring fluency.

LEHEN IKASGAIA — LESSON 1
HIZTEGIA — VOCABULARY

ama	mother	familia	family
aita	father	etxekoak	everyone at home
amona	grandmother	senide	near relative
aitona	grandfather	ahaide	distant relative
alaba	daughter	hil	die
seme	son	bizi	live
ahizpa	sister	etorri	come
anaia	brother	joan	go
izeba	aunt	eta	and
osaba	uncle	ez	no/neither... nor
loba	niece/nephew	lehen	before/earlier/used to...
iloba	grandchild	orain	now
lehengusina	cousin (female)	gero	later/then/later on
lehengusu	cousin (male)	aldi	time/tense
		nor	who?
		zer	what?

ADITZA — VERB
Izan - be

NOR

Indikatibozko orainaldia

ni naiz	I am
hi haiz	you are
hura da	he/she/it is
gu gara	we are
zu zara	you (singular) are
zuek zarete	you (plural) are
haik dira	they are

Indikatibozko lehenaldia

ni nintzen	I was
hi hintzen	you were
hura zen	he/she/it was
gu ginen	we were
zu zinen	you (sing.) were
zuek zineten	you (pl.) were
haik ziren	they were

OHARRA.—Bearing in mind that many native speakers of Basque do not use the "thou" form at all, and in the interests of keeping this Method as brief as possible, we shall present only the simplest verbal forms of "hi" (thou). As we said, many Basques use only the form "zu" (= you) when speaking to a second person. When speaking directly to more than one person, "zuek" (= you plural, "you all") is used.

*T.N.: Since the pronoun "thou" and its respective forms are considered archaic in English, the forms in "Hika" will be translated as "you". The student must simply remember that this is a more intimate way of speaking to a second person, similar to the Spanish or French "tu".

GRAMATIK ERREGELAK

ARTIKULUA.– The definite article ("the") for singular nouns is the suffix "-a" (without distinction of grammatical gender). If the noun without article ends in "a", no suffix is necessary. If the noun is plural, the suffix "-ak" is added. Thus: **ama, amak; semea, semeak.**

(T.N.: In Basque, any noun can be used in its generic sense without an article. While in English it is necessary to say "You are a/the son" or "You are my son", in Basque the determiner is not necessary. Thus, Zu seme zara. The possessive adjective (my, your, etc.) will, however, be indicated in parentheses in the translation where necessary. See also T.N., Lesson 8, gramatik erregelak.)

ADITZA.– Except for eleven verbs, all the others are conjugated with the help of an auxiliary, which follows the main verb in affirmative and interrogative sentences. Thus: I live = **ni bizi naiz,** he died = **hura hil zen.** The auxiliary is what is really conjugated, and indicates approximately the time and mode of action. For negative sentences, the word-order is modified, and the auxiliary goes before the main verb. Thus: I am not living = **ni ez naiz bizi;** he didn't die = **hura ez zen hil.**

ARIKETAK – EXERCISES

Ni alaba naiz. Zu semea zara.	I am the daughter. You are the son.
Ni alaba naiz. Zu seme zara	I am (the) daughter. You are (the) son.
Alaba naiz. Seme zara	I am (a) daughter. You are (a) son.
Aita eta ama etorri dira.	Father and Mother have come.
Izeba eta osaba etorri ziren.	(My) aunt and uncle came.
Zu eta biok joan ginen.	You and I went.
Aitona eta zu etorri zineten.	(Your) grandfather and you came.
Orain etorri zarete.	Now you have come.
Lehen etorri zen.	He came earlier.
Lehen bizi ziren.	They used to be alive. (Before, they lived).
Orain hil dira.	Now they are dead. (Now they have died).
Iloba ez da etorri.	The grandchild has not come.
Amona ez zen hil. Bizi da.	Grandmother didn't die. She's alive.
Ahizpa eta ni ez ginen etorri.	Sister and I didn't come.
Lehengusua eta zu ez zineten joan.	(Your) cousin and you didn't go.

BIGARREN IKASGAIA – LESSON TWO
HIZTEGIA – VOCABULARY

etxe	house		**mutil**	boy
estaia	apartment		**mutiko**	little boy
ate	door		**haur, ume**	child
eskailera	stairs		**berri**	new
leiho	window		**zahar**	old
mahai	table		**handi**	big/large
ohe	bed		**ttiki**	small/little
eserleku (aulki)	chair		**zabal**	wide
gela	room		**hestu**	narrow
sukalde	kitchen		**merke**	cheap
jantoki	dining room		**garesti**	expensive
komuna	W.C.		**hau, hauk**	he, she, it, this/they, these
bainu	bathroom		**hori, horik**	he, she, it, that/they, those
andre,emakume	woman	*	**hura, haik**	he, she, it, that/they, those
gizon	man		**apurtu**	break
neska	girl		**konpondu**	fix
neskato	little girl		**bat**	a/an; one (number)

ADITZA – VERBO

Indikatibozko gero aldia

The future tense is formed by adding the suffix "-ko" to the main verb which is then conjugated with the help of the auxiliary in the present tense. The main verb suffers no other change than the addition of the suffix "-ko" in this tense. Thus: ni biziko naiz (= I shall live); zu etorriko zara (= you will come). When the main verb ends in "n" or "l", the suffix "-go" is added instead of "-ko". Thus: Gu hil egingo gara (= we shall die).

Potentziala

In order to form the conditional, the same suffix is added as for the future, but the auxiliary verb is conjugated in the past tense. Thus: ni biziko nintzen (= I would live); zu etorriko zinen (= you would come); gu hilgo ginen (= we would die).

*T.N.: Hura, haik: While in English only two relationships of distance are expressed by the demonstratives "this" and "that", in Basque three such relationships exist. "Hura", and the plural "haik" are envisioned as further removed from the speaker than "hori, horik" (that, those). This difference, while untranslatable, must be borne in mind by the student.

GRAMATIK ERREGELAK

HITZEN EBAKITZEA (Pronunciation).

PRONUNCIATION:

The vowels, dipthongs and consonants which might cause difficulties for the English-speaking student, have been transcribed as follows in phonetic script:

A	[a]	EU	[eu]	G	[g]	TX	[tʃ]
E	[e]	AI	[ai]	S	[ş]	TZ	[ts]
I	[i]	EI	[ei]	Z	[s]		
O	[o]	OI	[oi]	X	[ʃ]		
U	[u]	J	[j]	TT	[tj]		
AU	[au]	H	[h]	TS	[tş]		

ARTIKULUA.— When a noun is followed by an adjective, it is the adjective which takes the article. Thus: the new house = **etxe berria;** the old men = **gizon zaharrak.**

ARIKETAK — EXERCISES

Mahaia apurtu zen.	The table was broken.*
Gero konponduko da	Later, it will be fixed.
Mahai hori apurtu zen.	That table was broken.
Ohe hori apurtuko da.	That bed will be broken.
Jantoki handia.	The large dining room.
Jantokia handia da.	The dining room is large. (...is a large one).
Bainua eta sukaldea ttikiak ziren	The bathroom and the kitchen were small.
Lehen haur ttiki bat zinen	You used to be a little child.
Gero gizon handi bat izango zara.	Later on, you will be a big man.
Atea zabala izango da.	The door will be wide. (...a wide one).
Mailadia hestua zen.	The staircase was narrow.
Etxe haik handiak izango dira.	Those houses will be large. (...large ones).
Handiak eta merkeak izango dira.	They will be large and cheap.
Etxe haik ez dira garestiak izango.	Those houses won't be expensive.
Bainua eta sukaldea ez dira handiak.	The bathroom and the kitchen aren't large.
Komuna ez da zaharra.	The w.c. isn't old.
Etxe zahar eta handia.	The old and large house.
Etxea zaharra eta handia da	The house is old and large.
Etxe hori zaharra eta handia da	That house is old and large.
Etxe hori ez da berria ez txikia.	That house is neither new nor small.
Mahaia ez da berria ez merkea.	The table is neither new nor cleap.

* T.N.: See Translators Note, Lesson 35, Ariketak.

HIRUGARREN IKASGAIA — LESSON THREE

HIZTEGIA

herri	town/village	gaur	today
hiri	city	bihar	tomorrow
bide	road/way	atzo	yesterday
autobide	highway	etzi	the day after tomorrow
• kale	street	arin, azkar	quickly, lively
espaloi	sidewalk	berandu	late
atezain	doorman	ikusi	see
zuhaitz	tree	jaiki	get up/rise
argi	light/bright	jaitsi	descend/get down, off
ilun	dark	egin	make/do
eguzki	sun	-(e)tik	from, through, around, along, out, of, off, etc.
hilargi	moon		
egun	day	-(e)ra	to
goiz	morning	erosi	buy
arratsalde	afternoon	saldu	sell
arrats	evening	trukatu	exchange/change
gau	night		

ADITZA NORK ZER
UKAN — HAVE

Indikatibozko orainaldia

nik	dut	ditut	I have
hik	duk, dun	dituk, ditun	you have
hark	du	ditu	he, she, it has
guk	dugu	ditugu	we have
zuk	duzu	dituzu	you (sing.) have
zuek	duzue	dituzue	you (pl.) have
haiek	dute	dituzte	they have

OHARRA.—For the forms in "hika", see OHARRA, LESSON 9, below.

•T.N.: "Kale", besides meaning "street", also means "outside" or "in town" as opposed to being in the country or on the farm.

GRAMATIK ERREGELAK

ARTIKULUA.— In the first lesson we said that the singular and plural articles were formed, respectively, by the suffixes "-a" and "-ak". This, however, is true only when the noun is the subject of an intransitive verb. If the noun is the subject of a transitive verb, the singular article is "-ak" and the plural is "-ek". Thus:

The man has seen the tree = **Gizonak zuhaitza ikusi du.**

The man has seen the trees = **Gizonak zuhaitzak ikusi ditu.**

The men have seen the tree = **Gizonek zuhaitza ikusi dute.**

The men have seen the trees = **Gizonek zuhaitzak ikusi dituzte.**

ADITZA.— On the preceding page, the verbs appear in two columns: dut, etc. and ditut, etc. The verbs in the first column are used when the direct object of the verb is singular, while the second column is for plural direct objects. (See examples above).

ARIKETAK

Ohetik jaiki eta kalera joan naiz	I've gotten up (out of bed) and gone to the street.
Lehen ohetik jaiki ginen.	We got up (out of bed) earlier.
Orain kalera joan gara.	Now we have gone to the street.
Gero hirira joango gara	Later, we'll go to the city.
Gizonak atea egin du	The man has made the door.
Anaiek mahaia egin dute	The brothers have made the table.
Aitak leihoak egin ditu	Father has made the windows.
Lehengusuek etxeak egin dituzte	The cousins have made the houses.
Etxetik jaitsi eta kalera joan zinen	You went down out of the house and into the street (You descended from the house and went to the street).
Anaia eta zu autobidetik joan zineten	(Your) brother and you took the highway. (...went along the highway)
Etxera etorri ginen	We came home (...to the house)
Eguzkia ikusi dugu	We have seen the sun.
Hilargia eta izarrak ikusi dituzue	You have seen the moon and the stars.
Lehen goiza zen. Orain arratsaldea da	It used to be morning. Now it is (the) afternoon
Gero gaua izango da	Later on, it will be night.
Bihar berandu izango da	Tomorrow will be (too) late.

OHARRA.— Notice that "bat" always follows the noun, and that the rest of the numbers precede it. Thus: **mahai bat, bi mahai, hiru mahai.**

LAUGARREN IKASGAIA — LESSON FOUR

HIZTEGIA

ikastola	school	kolore	colour
ikastetxe	school	zuri	white
ikasgela	classroom	gris	gray
irakasle	teacher	beltz	black
ikasle	student	laranja	orange
maisu	school master	gorri	red
maistra	school mistress	more	violet
andereño	school teacher (female)	berde	green
harbel	blackboard	karmin	scarlet
asko	much/many/a lot	urdin	blue
gutti	little/few	xipiroi	squid
on	good	hori	yellow
txar	bad	oliba	olive
ongi	well (adv.)	egon	be
txarto, gaizki	badly/the wrong way	irten	leave/go out
gaizto	bad (people)	sartu	enter/go in/take in
hemen(txe)	(right) here	non	where?
hor(txe)	(right) there	zenbat	how many/much?
han(txe)	(right) over there	-(e)an	in/on/inside/at/during

ADITZA: UKAN (NORK-ZER)

Indikatibozko lehenaldia

nik	nuen	nituen	I had
hik	huen	hituen	you had
hark	zuen	zituen	he had
guk	genuen	genituen	we had
zuk	zenuen	zenituen	you (sing.) had
zuek	zenuten	zenituzten	you (pl.) had
haiek	zuten	zituzten	they had

OHARRA.—*In negative sentences, the word order changes. Thus:*
  nik ikusi nuen
  nik ez nuen ikusi

In interrogative sentences, the subject usually goes at the end. Thus:
  nik ikusi nuen
  ikusi nuen nik?

ARIKETAK

Ikastolara joan naiz	I have gone to (the) school.
Anaia unibertsitatera joan da	(My) brother has gone to the university.
Irakaslea ikusi dut	I've seen the teacher.
Andereñoak ez dira etorri	The schoolteachers haven't come.
Andoni maisua ez Miren andereñoa ez ditut ikusi	I haven't seen Anthony, the schoolmaster, nor Mary, the schoolteacher.
Ikasleak ikusi genituen	We saw the students.
Ikusi zenituzten ikasleak?	Did you see the students?
Ikasleak ez genituen ikusi	We did not see the students.
Maisuak lapitzak hartu zituen	The teacher took the pencils.
Ikasleak ez zituen hartu lapitzak	The student didn't take the pencils.
Hartu genituen guk lapitzak?	Did we take the pencils?
Etxe handiak ikusi ditut	I've seen the big houses.
Ikusi ditut etxe handiak?	Have I seen the big houses?
Etxe handiak ez ditut ikusi	I haven't seen the big houses.
Irakasleak ikastolara joan ziren	The teachers went to (the) school.
Joan ginen ikasleak unibertsitatera?	Have we (students) gone to the university?
Maisuak ez ziren ikastolara joan	The teachers didn't go to the school.
Hori ikasle txarra da	He is a bad student.
Ikasle txarra da Ander?	Is Andrew a bad student?
Ander ez da gizon gaiztoa.	Andrew is not a bad man.
Hori gaizki egin duzu	You havent done that well. (You've done that badly).
Etxea garesti erosi zenuten	You bought that house at a high cost.
Lapitzak trukatu zituzten	They exchanged the pencils.
Autobusa hartu genuen	We caught (took) the bus.
Boligrafoak merke erosi zituzten	They bought the ballpoint pens cheap.
Hantxe ikusi dut	I saw him right over there.
Hementxe etorri da	He has come right to this spot.

BOSTGARREN IKASGAIA — LESSON FIVE

HIZTEGIA

zero (huts)	0	hogei eta hamar	30
bat	1	hogei eta hamaika	31
bi	2	berrogei	40
hiru	3	berrogei eta hiru	43
lau	4	berrogeietahamar	50
bost	5	hirurogei	60
sei	6	hirurogei eta hamar	70
zazpi	7	laurogei	80
zortzi	8	laurogei eta hamar	90
bederatzi	9	ehun	100
hamar	10	berrehun	200
hamaika	11	hirurehun	300
hamabi	12	laurehun	400
hamahiru	13	bostehun	500
hamalau	14	seirehun	600
hamabost	15	zazpirehun	700
hamasei	16	zortzirehun	800
hamazazpi	17	bederatzirehun	900
hamazortzi	18	mila	1.000
hemeretzi	19	miliar	1.000.000.000
hogei	20	milioi	1.000.000
hogei eta bat	21		

ADITZ SINTETIKOA: EGON — BE
THERE IS, THERE ARE

Indikatibozko orainaldia

ni nago	I am
hi hago	you are
hura dago	he is/there is
gu gaude	we are
zu zaude	you are
zuek zaudete	you are
haik daude	they are/there are

Indikatibozko lehenaldia

ni nengoen	I was
hi hengoen	you were
hura zegoen	he was/there was
gu geunden	we were
zu zeunden	you were
zuek zeundeten	you were
haik zeuden	they were/there were

GRAMATIK ERREGELAK

Nouns accompanied by numbers are always used in the singular. Thus: **hiru seme** = three sons. The verb which follows can either be used in the singular or in the plural. Thus: **hiru gizon ikusi nuen** (= **hiru gizon ikusi nituen**) = I saw three men. "Bat" (one) follows the noun, while all other numbers precede it: **gizon bat, bi gizon, hiru gizon,** etc.

ARIKETAK

Ni hemen nago	I am here.
Zuek han zeundeten	You were there.
Non geunden gu?	Where were we?
Gu etxean geunden	We were at home.
Non zeuden ikasleak?	Where were the students?
Ikasleak ikastolan zeuden	The students were in the school.
Non zeunden?	Where were you?
Komunean zeunden	You were in the w.c.
Non zegoen aita?	Where was Father?
Aita kalean ikusi nuen	I saw father in the street. (outside).
Non zeuden irakasleak?	Where were the teachers?
Irakasleak ikasgelan ikusi nituen	I saw the teachers in the classroom.
Non zeuden?. Non zeunden?	Where were they? Where were you?
Hamalau andre eta bost gizon zeundeten	There were 14 women and 5 men (of you).
Mila bederatzirehun eta hirurogei eta sei	One thousand nine hundred and sixty-six.
Ehun zuhaitz handi zeuden han. (= zegoen han)	There were a hundred big trees over there.
Etxe hark ate bat eta lau leiho ditu	That house has one door and four windows.
Han mahai zahar bat zegoen	There was an old table over there.
Lau eta bost bederatzi dira	Four and five is nine.
Gizon beltz bat ikusi nuen	I saw a black man.
Andre bat, bi andre, hiru andre	One woman, 2 women, 3 women.
Gizon bat, bi gizon, hiru gizon	One man, 2 men, 3 men
Bi anaïa, anaia bat	Two brothers, one (a) brother.

SEIGARREN IKASGAIA — LESSON SIX

HIZTEGIA

àste	week	gehiago	more
hilabete, hil	month	guttiago	less
urte	year	orratz	needle/hand (of a clock)
mende	century	erloju, ordulari	clock/watch
ordu	hour	beraz	so/therefore/thus
minutu	minute	zer	what?
segundu	second	urtarril	January
erdi	half/middle	otsail	February
laurden	quarter	martxo	March
udaberri	Spring	apiril	April
uda	Summer	maiatz	May
udazken	Fall	ekain	June
negu	Winter	uztail	July
haro	season	agorril	August
astelehen	Monday	irail	September
astearte	Tuesday	urri	October
asteazken	Wednesday	hazil	November
ostegun	Thursday	abendu	December
ostirale	Friday	Gabon	Christmas
larunbat	Saturday	Urte Berri	New Year's
igande	Sunday	hotz	cold
eguerdi	noon	bero	hot

ADITZ SINTETIKOA: JOAN — GO

Indikatibozko orainaldia

ni noa	I am going
hi hoa	you are going
hura doa	he is going
gu goaz	we are going
zu zoaz	you are going
zuek zoazte	you are going
haik doaz	they are going

Indikatibozko lehenaldia

ni nindoan	I was going
hi hindoan	you were going
hura zihoan	he was going
gu gindoazen	we were going
zu zindoazen	you were going
zuek zindoazten	you were going
haik zihoazen	they were going

ARIKETAK

Lehen neguan geunden	It used to be Winter. (Before, we were in Winter)
Abenduan geunden eta hotz zegoen	It was (we were in) December and it was cold.
Orain udan gaude eta bero dago	Now it is Summer and it is hot.
Gabonak abenduaren hogei eta bostean dira	Christmas is on the twenty-fifth of Dec.
Abenduaren 24ean Gabon Zaharra da	Christmas Eve is on December 24th.
Abenduaren hogei eta hamaikan Urte Zaharra da	New Year's Eve is on December 31st.
Urtarrilaren lehenean Urte Berria da	January first is New Year's Day.
Hogeigarren mendean gaude	We are in the Twentieth Century.
Urteak lau haro ditu	The year has four seasons.
Zer ordu da?	What time is it?
Hamarrak dira	It's ten o'clock.
Goizeko hirurak dira	It's three o'clock in the morning.
Gaueko hamarrak ziren	It was ten p.m.
Hiru t´erdiak	Three thirty.
Hirurak eta hamar	Three ten/ten past three.
Laurak hamar guttiago	Ten to four/three fifty.
Ordu batak dira	It's one o'clock.
Ordu batak eta laurdenak	A quarter past one/one fifteen
Zazpiak laurden guttiago	A quarter to seven
Orratz ttikia bian dago eta handia bostean	The small hand is on the two and the big one is on the five.
Beraz, ordu biak eta hogeitabost dira	So, it's two twenty-five.
Bostak eta laurdenetan joango naiz	I'll go at five fifteen.
Seiak hamar guttiagotan etorri zen	He came at ten to six.
Otsailaren hogeia	February 20th.
Donostian, mila bederatziehun eta hirurogei eta hamasei garreneko ekainaren hogei eta seian.	(In) San Sebastian, June 26, 1976.

ZAZPIGARREN IKASGAIA — LESSON SEVEN

HIZTEGIA

euri	rain	euritako	umbrella
elur	snow	eguzkitako	parasol
txingor	hail	belar	grass
kazkabar	hail	lore	flower
izotz	frost/frozen	arrosa	rose
ihintz	dew	krabelin	carnation
hodei	cloud	jeranio	geranium
laino	fog	nor, nortzu	Who? (sing., pl.)
ekaitz	storm	zein, zeintzu	Which? (sing., pl.)
trumoi	thunder	nola?	How?/What's... like?/Why?
tximist	lightning	bezala	like/as
busti	get wet/dampen	hasi	begin/start
lehor	dry (adj.)	esan	say/tell
hitz	word	arte	between/among/until
hitz egin	speak/talk		
esaldi	sentence/phrase		

ADITZ SINTETIKOA: ETORRI — COME

Indikatibozko orainaldia

ni nator	I am coming
hi hator	you are coming
hura dator	he is coming
gu gatoz	we are coming
zu zatoz	you are coming
zuek zatozte	you are coming
haik datoz	they are coming

Indikatibozko lehenaldia

ni nentorren	I was coming
hi hentorren	you were coming
hura zetorren	he was coming
gu gentozen	we were coming
zu zentozen	you were coming
zuek zentozten	you were coming
haik zetozen	they were coming

ARIKETAK

Gaur euria da
Today it's raining.

Kalea busti egin da
The street is wet. (...has become wet)

Atzo elurra zegoen
Yesterday there was snow.

Atzo elurra zen
Yesterday it was snowing.

Mendiak eta zelaiak zuri zeuden
The mountains and fields were white.

Uda joan da
Summer has gone.

Negua etorri da
Winter has come.

Ez da bero. Hotz da
It isn't hot. It's cold.

Trumoiak eta tximistak daude
There is thunder and lightning.

Ekaitza etorri da
The storm has come.

Loreak bustirik zeuden
The flowers were wet.

Belarrek ihintza zuten
The grass(es) had dew on it (them).

Nor etorri da?
Who has come?

Aita joan zen
Father went out (away).

Atezaina atean zegoen
The doorman was in the doorway.

Mendira gindoazen
We were going to the mountain. (country).

Etxetik gentozen
We were coming from home.

Nora zindoazen?
Where were you going?

Zuek zindoazten eta haik zetozen
You were going and they were coming.

Goizean euria zen
It rained this morning. (in the morning).

Hodeiak joan dira eta orain eguzkia dago
The clouds have gone and now it is sunny. (there is sun)

Gauean hilargia egongo da
Tonight there will be a moon.

Lore bi ikusi ditut: arrosa gorri bat eta krabelin zuria
I've seen two flowers: a red rose and a white carnation.

Portugal-eko krabelin gorriak
The red carnations of Portugal.

Euskal Herriko mendi berde eta zelai horiak
The green hills and yellow fields of the Basque Country.

Bretaina Handiko zeru iluna
The dark sky of Great Britain.

Alemaniako hiri industrialak
The industrial cities of Germany.

ZORTZIGARREN IKASGAIA — LESSON EIGHT

HIZTEGIA

lantoki	place of work		**larru**	skin
langile	worker		**aurpegi**	face
bulego	office		**buru**	head
morroi	servant		**begi**	eye
nagusi	boss		**sudur**	nose
ugazaba	owner		**aho**	mouth
erreminta	tool		**belarri**	ear
fabrika	factory		**kokots**	chin
makina	machine		**hatzamar**	finger
mailu	hammer		**esku**	hand
iltze	nail		**beso**	arm
atera	remove/take out		**hatzazal**	fingernail
gogor	strong/hard		**oin**	foot
bigun	soft		**izter**	thigh
leun	smooth		**ipurdi**	bottom
aurre	ahead/in front of		**bular**	chest
atze	behind/in back of		**lepo**	back/shoulders
bai	yes		**belaun**	knee
etzi	day after tomorrow		**ari izan**	be doing/involved in
etsi	be bored/fed up			

ADITZ SINTETIKOA: IBILI — WALK*

Indikatibozko orainaldia

ni nabil	I am walking
hi habil	you are walking
hura dabil	he is walking
gu gabiltza	we are walking
zu zabiltza	you are walking
zuek zabiltzate	you are walking
haik dabiltza	they are walking

Indikatibozko lehenaldia

ni nenbilen	I was walking
hi henbilen	you were walking
hura zebilen	he was walking
gu genbiltzan	we were walking
zu zenbiltzan	you were walking
zuek zenbiltza ten	you were walking
haik zebiltzan	they were walking

* Translator's note: "Ibili" literally means "walk", but it is a verb with many figurative uses, the most general of which might be translated as "get on (in life)". Thus, the common greeting: Nola zabiltza? (= How are you/How are things?) Often, this verb can only be translated as "be/be around", as in the question, "Zenbat zabiltzate ikastolan?" (= How many of you are at school?)

GRAMATIK ERREGELAK

The subject of a transitive verb always bears the suffix "-k". Thus: **nor da?** = Who is it? (intransitive verb); **nork egin du?** = Who has done it? (transitive verb).*

The past participle (for use as a qualifier, but not for forming the perfect tenses — T.N.) is made by adding the suffix "-ta" to the verb. Thus: **apurtuta** = broken. By adding the suffix "-t(z)en", the gerund or present participle is formed. Thus: **apurtzen** = breaking.

By adding the suffix "-rik" to a verb, a type of past participle (again for adjectival use — T.N.) is obtained. Thus: **apurturik** = broken. When the same suffix is added to a noun, the latter is understood in its most generic sense and does not refer to any particular example of its class. (This suffix is most often used in interrogative and negative sentences, and can often be translated as "any/some/no". Thus: **ez dago ogirik** = there isn't any bread.—T.N.)

By adding the suffix "-a" to a verb, a noun or adjective can be obtained. Thus: **apurtua** = the broken thing/one; **aulki apurtua** = the broken chair. (In this last example, "apurtua" is a true adjective and can be pluralized: **aulki apurtuak** = the broken chairs; while "apurtuta", considered as a participle, cannot.—T.N.)

ARIKETAK

Nork erosi zituen etxe horik?	Who bought those houses?
Zeintzu etxe?. Horik?. Bai, horik	Which houses? Those ones? Yes, those.
Bustirik zaude. Bustita zaudete	You are wet. You (pl.) are wet.
Neskak mutila ikusi zuen	The girl saw the boy.
Nola zabiltzate?	How are things? (see note, preceding page).
Lehen bezala gabiltza	Same as always.
Nola zaudete bustirik?	How come you're wet?
Atzo ez zegoen esnerik	Yesterday there wasn't any milk.
Gizon hila eta mutil bizia ikusi ditut	I've seen the dead man and the live boy.
Aho bat eta begi bi ditugu	We have one mouth and two eyes.
Zu asko zenbiltzan	You were walking a lot.
Nagusia fabrikatik bulegora joan da	The boss has gone from the factory to the office.
Eskuak bost hatzamar ditu	The hand has five fingers.
Hatzamarrak hatzazal bat du	The finger has a nail.

*T.N.—For help in distinguishing transitive and intransitive main verbs, remember that whenever the auxiliary UKAN is used, the action is considered transitive, and the subject of the verb must end in "-k": NORK. When the auxiliary is IZAN, the verb is considered intransitive and its subject is NOR.

BEDERATZIGARREN IKASGAIA – LESSON NINE

HIZTEGIA

balio	be worth	aulki	chair/bench
alkate	mayor	baizik	but/rather
alkondara	shirt	bakarrik	only/alone
jaso	lift/raise	baserri	farm
gertatu	happen	barru	inside/interior
ardo	wine	baserritar	farmer
edan	drink (verb)	baso	woods/forest
ezpain	lip	bazkari	lunch
hortz	tooth	afari	dinner
mihi	tongue	bazkaldu	eat lunch
eztarri	throat	afaldu	eat dinner
idun	neck	jan	eat
ile	hair	begiratu	watch/look at
arraultze	egg	behi	cow
frijitu	fried	idi	steer
artaziak	scissors	beltzaran	brunette/dark complexioned
zarata	noise	atsegin	like/please

ADITZ SINTETIKOA: EDUKI – TENER

Indikatibozko orainaldia

nik daukat	I have
hik daukak-n	you have
hark dauka	he has
guk daukagu	we have
zuk daukazu	you have
zuek daukazue	you have
haiek daukate	they have

Indikatibozko lehenaldia

nik neukan	I had
hik heukan	you had
hark zeukan	he had
guk geneukan	we had
zuk zeneukan	you had
zuek zeneukaten	you had
haiek zeukaten	they had

OHARRA.—Notice that in the "hik" (thou/you) form, the verb ends in "k-n" in the present tense. The "k" is used when speaking to a man, and the "n" when speaking to a woman. Thus: poltsikoan daukak = You have it in (your) pocket (You, a boy or man, have it). But: poltsikoak daukan = You (a girl) have it in your pocket.

GRAMATIK ERREGELAK

The verb UKAN, studied in the third lesson, and the verb EDUKI, which is presented in this ninth lesson, are distinguished in their use as follows: The verb UKAN is above all the auxiliary for all transitive verbs; used as a main verb, however, its meaning is "have" when the object of the verb is not kept or carried in any particular space. Thus: **nik begiak ditut** = I have eyes (but I don't specify their being enclosed within something else). EDUKI is used when we keep or carry the object inside something. Thus: **buruan ideia bat daukat** = I have an idea in my head. However: **buruan ileak ditut** = I have hair on my head.

The suffix "-ri" for singular nouns ending in a vowel often corresponds to the preposition "at/to", or signals an indirect object (singular) when the noun ends in a vowel. Thus: **amari** = (Give) mother (the book). However, if we wish to include the article (or other determiner, the/a/my, etc.), the suffix is "-ari". Thus: **gizonari** = (Give) the man (the book).

The suffix "-ei" signals a plural indirect object in all cases. Thus: **gizonei** = to (the) men; **ikasleei** = to (the) students.

The suffix "-ra" is used when we wish to indicate that we are going to a place. Thus: **etxera** = to the house. If the word ends in a consonant, the suffix is "-era". Thus: **harbelera** = to the blackboard. The plural suffix is "-(e)tara". Thus: **etxeetara** = to the houses.

Whenever suffixes are added, the following must be borne in mind: if the noun ends in a vowel, and the suffix also begins with a vowel, both vowels conform to the following rule: A + A = A; A + E = E; E + E = EE. Thus: **amei** = to the mothers.

ARIKETAK

Begira harbelari	Look at the blackboard.
Harbelera goaz	We're going to the blackboard.
Ez begira etxeei	Don't look at the houses.
Etxeetara zindoazten	You were going to the houses.
Besoa jaso eta ardoa edan nuen	I raised my arm and drank the wine.
Zer jaso duzu?. Oina	What have you lifted? (My) foot.
Zer gertatu da?. Gauza asko gertatu da	What has happened? Many things have happened
Afaldu duzu gaur?. Ez, gaur ez dut afaldu	Have you had dinner? No, today I havent eaten dinner.
Baserritarra baserrira joan zen	The farmer went to the farm.
Bihar mendietara joango gara	Tomorrow we'll go to the mountains.
Atsegin dut arraultze frijitua	I like fried egg(s).
Arraultze frijituak atsegin ditut	I like fried eggs.

HAMARGARREN IKASGAIA – LESSON TEN

HIZTEGIA

berehala	right now/immediately	egunero	every day
berezi	special	eguraldi	weather
betaurrekoak	eyeglasses	eliza	church
bibote	mustache	apez	priest
bizar	beard	erretore	parish priest
bota	throw (verb)	apezpiku	bishop
botila	bottle	elkar	together/each other
burdina	iron (metal)	elkarrizketa	conversation
harri	stone	senargai	boyfriend
ikatz	coal	emaztegai	girlfriend
ebaki	cut (verb)	senar	husband
edari	drink (noun)	emazte	wife
eder	beautiful	epel	warm
polit	pretty	erabili	use/utilize
ohitura	custom	ere	also/too
okela	meat	berriz ere	again/another time
egosi	braise/stew	erre	burn

ADITZ SINTETIKOA: JAKIN – KNOW

Indikatibozko orainaldia

nik dakit	I know
hik dakik-n	you know
hark daki	he knows
guk dakigu	we know
zuk dakizu	you know
zuek dakizue	you know
haiek dakite	they know

Indikatibozko lehenaldia

nik nekien	I knew
hik hekien	you knew
hark zekien	he knew
guk genekien	we knew
zuk zenekien	you knew
zuek zenekiten	you knew
haiek zekiten	they knew

GRAMATIK ERREGELAK

The suffix "-aren", when added to a noun in the singular (whether animate or inanimate), indicates possession.

* The suffix "-(e)ko", when added to inanimate nouns in the singular, corresponds to the English prepositions "of/from/in" and indicates a relationship of place.

The suffix "-en" is the plural of "-aren".

The suffix "-etako" is the plural of "-ko".

ARIKETAK

Etxe hori irakaslearena da	This house is the teacher's.
Mendietako zuhaitzak asko ziren	The trees of the mountains were many.
Baserriko atea	The door of the farmhouse. (The farm door).
Baserriko atearen kolorea	The color of the farmhouse door.
Aitaren baserriko atearen kolorea	The color of father's farmhouse door. (The color of the door of Father's farm).
Trumoien zarata handia zen	The thunder made a loud noise. (The noise of the thunder was great).
Gizonaren bibotearen kolore beltza	The black color of the man's mustache.
Ederrak ziren emaztearen ileak	The woman's hair was beautiful.
Elizako apezak etorri ziren	The priests of the church came.
Ez genekien hori	We didn't know that.
Botilako ura beroa zegoen	The water of the bottle was hot.
Eguraldi epela dago	The weather is warm.
Fabriketako langileen tresnak	The factory workers' tools.
Egosi zenuen okela?	Did you braise the meat?
Nola da herriko ohitura zahar hori?	What is that old village custom like?
Elizako apezen elkarrizketa	The conversation of the priests of the church.
Senarrak bizarra eta bibotea ebaki egin ditu	The husband has cut his beard and mustache.
Alkatearen ahoko hortzak	The teeth of (in) the Mayor's mouth.
Agur, bihar arte	Good-bye, see you (until) tomorrow.
Etzirarte	Until the day after tomorrow.
Etsita nago. Nola zaude?. Etsita. Etsirik	I'm fed up. How are you? Tired. Bored/fed up.

* T.N.—When the suffix "-KO" is added to a place name, the latter becomes an adjective: Ameriketako jendeak = the American people.

HAMAIKAGARREN IKASGAIA – LESSON ELEVEN

HIZTEGIA

esaera	phrase	giltza	key
eskaini	offer (verb)	habia	nest
etorkizun	future	txori	bird
ezagutu	know	gona	skirt
ezin izan/ukan	not be able/can't	galtzerdi	sock
ahal izan/ukan	be able/can	gorde	keep/put away
filme	film/movie	haizkora	axe
fruitu	fruit	gose	hunger
gain	on/above/upper	goze izan	be hungry
azpi	under/lower/beneath	gurasoak	parents
goi	. up	gurutze	cross (noun)
behe	down	guzti	all/every
galdera	question	haritz	oak
galdetu	ask	hartu	take/get
erantzun	answer	eman	give
garbi	clean (adj.)	sineste	belief
zikin	dirty	sinetsi	believe
		maitatu	love (verb)
		maite ukan	love (verb)
		maitasun	love (noun)

ADITZ SINTETIKOA: ESAN — SAY/TELL

Indikatibozko orainaldia

nik diot	I am saying
hik diok-n	you are saying
hark dio	he is saying
guk diogu	we are saying
zuk diozu	you are saying
zuek diozue	you are saying
haiek diote	they are saying

Indikatibozko lehenaldia

nik nioen	I was saying
hik hioen	you were saying
hark zioen	he was saying
guk genion	we were saying
zuk zenioen	you were saying
zuek zenioten	you were saying
haiek zioten	they were saying

GRAMATIK ERREGELAK

The suffix "-arengan" is used for living beings, in the singular. The plural suffix is "-engan". It denotes those persons in whom we have deposited belief, hope, love, etc. (Thus, nouns bearing this suffix are usually the objects of verbs of feeling or belief, and in English translation may often be preceded by prepositions such as "in/for".–T.N.)

* The suffix "-(e)an" is for inanimate objects in the singular; the plural is "-etan". This suffix tells us where something is, and corresponds to the English prepositions "in/on/inside/at, etc.

ARIKETAK

Zer duzu hor gainean?. Ileak	What do you have up there? Hair.
Zein dago han goian?. Txoria	What is up there? The bird.
Habia gain hori zikirr dago	That upper part of the nest is dirty.
Mahai azpi hori ez dago garbi	That lower part of the table isn't clean. (It isn't clean underneath the table).
Semea ohe azpian sartu zen	My son got underneath the bed.
Gizon horiek etxe horik erosi zituzten	Those men bought those houses.
Ostirale arratsaldean etorriko naiz	I'll come on Friday afternoon.
Larunbat goizean joan ginen	We went on Saturday morning.
Zenbat zabiltzate ikastolan?	How many (students) are you at school?
Bostehun bat gabiltza ikastolan	There are about 500 of us at school.
Ohe hau aita eta amarena da	This bed is Father and Mother's.
Izebaren aulki zabala	My aunt's wide chair.
Amarengan dut maitasuna	I feel love for my mother. (I have love for/in...).
Gizonengan sinesten dut	I believe in mankind.
Hilargirako bidea luzea da	It's a long way to the moon.
Menditik hirira etorri nintzen	I came from the mountain to the city.
Etxeko komunaren atea zaharra zen	The bathroom door of the house was old.
Lehengusuaren ikastolako leihoak handiak dira	My cousin's school's windows (the windows in my cousins school) are big.
Belar berdearen kolorea polita zen	The green color of the grass was pretty.
Gizon handiaren gela zabala da	The large man's room is wide.
Zer dakizu?. Gauza asko dakit	What do you know? I know many things.
Semeek ez dakite gauza askorik	My sons don't know many things.
Gero azkar ikasiko dituzte	Later on, they will learn quickly.
Zelaiko loreak bustirik daude	The flowers in the field are wet.
Kale zabaleko zuhaitzak ikusi nituen	I saw the trees in the wide street
Gizonek gizonak ikusi zituzten	The men saw the men.
Izebaren alaben etxeak asko ziren	My aunt's daughters'houses were many.

HAMABIGARREN IKASGAIA — LESSON TWELVE

HIZTEGIA

haize	wind/air	hibai	river
harrapatu	catch	aberastasun	wealth/riches
haserretu	get angry	aberats	rich person
haserre	anger	aberastu	get rich
pozik	happy	gozo	sweet/tasty
poztu	get/be happy	txiro, pobre	poor
		pobretasun	poverty
hazi	grow	bigun, lehun	soft
hegazkin	airplane	latz	rough
heldu	arrive	gogor	hard/strong
hertsi	close (verb)	bigundu, lehundu	soften
zabaldu	open/enlarge	laztu	roughen/toughen
hezur	bone	ahantzi	forget
mami	crumb	gogoratu	remember
larru	skin	gogora ekarri	remind
		lodi	fat
		mehe	thin

ADITZ SINTETIKOA: IKUSI — SEE

Indikatibozko orainaldia

nik dakusat	I see
hik dakusak-n	you see
hark dakusa	he sees
guk dakusagu	we see
zuk dakusazu	you see
zuek dakusazue	you see
haiek dakusate	they see

Indikatibozko lehenaldia

nik nekusan	I saw
hik hekusan	you saw
hark zekusan	he saw
guk genekusan	we saw
zuk zenekusan	you saw
zuek zenekusaten	you saw
haiek zekusaton	they saw

OHARRA.—Many of the "synthetic" verbs which we have been studying in these lessons are also frequently conjungated with auxiliary verbs. Thus, nik dakusat and nik ikusten dut; gu gindoazen and gu joaten ginen can be used indifferently. However, the synthetic form is a much more precise indicator of tense.

(T.N.: In the present tense, the synthetic form corresponds to the ARI IZAN, or English present continuous, and indicates what is happening now, as opposed to the present simple, which tells us what usually happens).

GRAMATIK ERREGELAK

The preposition "for" (meaning for whom something is done or intended) is translated by adding the suffix "-arentzat" to animate nouns in the singular. Thus: **amarentzat.** The plural is "-entzat". Thus: **semeentzat.** For inanimate objects, the singular suffix is "-rako", and the plural is "-etarako".

"For" (meaning because of, due to, or in answer to the question why something is done) is indicated by the suffix "-arengatik". Thus: **amarengatik, gauzarengatik.** The plural is "-engatik". Thus: **semeengatik, etxeengatik.**

"With" (meaning in the company of whom or what something is done) is indicated by the suffix "-arekin". Thus: **amarekin, gauzarekin.** The plural is "-ekin". Thus: **semeekin, etxeekin.**

ARIKETAK

Zenbat dira etxeko gelak?	How many rooms are there in the house?
Eman andreari eserleku hori.	Give the woman that seat.
Eman andreei eserlekuak	Give the seats to (the) women.
Eman andreri eserlekuak	Give the seats to women.
Hiri handi bat dakusagu	We (can) see a big city. (are seeing...).
Gauetan hilargia genekusan (ikusten genuen)	At night, we (could) see the moon.
Eguzkiaren beroa handia zen	The sun was very hot. (the sun's heat was great).
Urtearen hilabeteak hamabi dira	There are twelve months in a year.
Astearen egunak zazpi dira	(The week's days are seven).
Urtaroak ez dira bost, lau dira	There aren't 5 seasons in a year, there are 4.
Goizeko argiaren kolorea	The color of the morning light.
Gaueko ilunaren kolore beltza	The black color of the darkness of night.
Uztaileko egun luze eta beroak	The long, hot days of July.
Uztaila urtearen zazpigarren hilabetea da	July is the seventh month of the year.
Euskal Herriko mendiak eta Euskal Herriaren izana	The mountains of the Basque Country and the Basque Country's being (character).
Mendiko zuhaitzak eta mendiaren izena	Mountain trees and the mountain's name.
Ikastolako ikasgelaren leihoak	The windows in the school classroom.
Gizonaren semearen lehengusua	The man's son's cousin.
Hirira autoan goaz	We're going to the city by car.
Unibertsitatera autobusean noa	I'm going to the University by bus.
Maisuak eta maistrek asko dakite	The teacher (male) and the teachers (female) know a lot.
Maisuek eta maistrak asko dakite	The teachers (male) and the teacher (female) know a lot.
Atzo gaueko hamarretan joan zineten	You left at ten last night.

HAMAHIRUGARREN IKASGAIA
LESSON THIRTEEN

HIZTEGIA

orma	wall	inon	somewhere/anywhere
huts	empty space	inon ez	nowhere/anywhere
hutsik	empty (adj.)	inor	someone/anyone
ibili	walk (see p. 18)	inor ez	no-one/anyone
ibilaldi	walk (noun)	irakurri	read
bidaia	trip	irakurgai	something to read
ibiltari	walker/hiker	irabazi	earn
bidaiari	traveler	galdu	lose
idatzi	write	bilatu	find
idazle	writer	irudi	drawing/image/likeness
idazti	text	itsaso	sea/ocean
liburu	book	hondartza	beach
eskutitz	letter	ur	water
ideia	idea	esne	milk
igon	go up/climb	itsasuntzi	boat
ikasi	learn/study	itsusi	ugly
inguru	around/near	labur	short
		moztu, ebaki	cut (verb)

ADITZ SINTETIKOA: EKARRI — BRING

Indikatibozko orainaldia

nik dakart	I am bringing
hik dakark-rren	you are bringing
hark dakar	he is bringing
guk dakargu	we are bringing
zuk dakarzu	you are bringing
zuek dakarzue	you are bringing
haiek dakarte	they are bringing

Indikatibozko lehenaldia

nik nekarren	I was bringing
hik hekarren	you were bringing
hark zekarren	he was bringing
guk genekarren	we were bringing
zuk zenekarren	you were bringing
zuek zenekarten	you were bringing
haiek zekarten	they were bringing

ARIKETAK

Nola ibili zinen?. Autoz	How did you come? By car.
Mendiz etorri ginen	We came cross-country. (...by way of...).
Gaur, udaz hitz egingo dugu	Today we'll talk about the summer.
Horik menditako loreak dira	Those are mountain flowers.
Gizon hori hiritara joaten da	That man goes to cities.
Andre hau ez doa hirietara	This woman doesn't go to the cities.
Andrez hitz egin zuten	They talked about women.
Menditik zelaira jaitsi nintzen	I came down from the mountain to the field.
Ohetik jaiki ginen. (atzo)	We got up. (yesterday).
Aitaren etxeko oheak berriak dira	The beds in Father's house are new (ones).
Menditako oihanetan zuhaitz asko dago	There are many trees in the mountain forests.
Abenduko gauetan hotz dago	December nights are cold. (It is cold on...).
Udako egunetan eguraldi beroa dago	On summer days, the weather is warm. (There is hot weather).
Gauza asko dakargu	We are bringing many things.
Gaurko egunak euria dakar	Today it will rain. (the day will bring...).
Gelako mahaiaren erdian	In the middle of the table in the room.
Etxeko gelako mahaiaren erdian	In the middle of the table of the room in the house.
Lehen ekarri genituen	We brought them before. (earlier).
Ikastolarako harbela nekarren	I brought the blackboard for the school.
Ikastolako harbelaren kolorea beltza da	The color of the school blackboard is black.
Mendietako loreen koloreak gorria, urdina eta morea dira	The colors of (the) mountain flowers are red, blue, and violet.
Menditako loreen koloreak	The colors of mountain flowers.
Menditako loreren koloreak	Mountain flower colors.
Mendiko lorearen kolorea	The mountain flower's color.
Astelehenetako arratsaldetan joango gara	We'll go on Monday afternoons.
Astelehen goizean etorriko naiz	I'll come on Monday morning.
Ostirale gauean ikusiko dut	I'll see him Friday night.
Igande eguerdian hirian geunden	We were in the city on Sunday at noon.

HAMALAUGARREN IKASGAIA
LESSON FOURTEEN
HIZTEGIA

denda	store/shop		**hibai**	river
dendari	salesperson/shop keeper		**ertz**	edge/shore
janari	food		**jantzi**	clothing/suit/dress
janaridenda	grocery store		**ipini**	put/put on
			kendu	remove/take off, out/get rid of
aparkaleku	parking place/lot		**hartu**	take/get/catch
liburudenda	book store		**harea**	sand
kafetegi	cafeteria		**sartu**	enter/take in
kutxa	box		**irten**	leave/go out
diru	money		**arrain**	fish
zaindu	keep/guard		**harategi**	butcher's/meat market
diruzain	cashier		**liburutegi**	library

ADITZ SINTETIKOA: ERAMAN — TAKE/CARRY
(away, out, etc.)

Indikatibozko orainaldia		**Indikatibozko lehenaldia**	
nik daramat	I am taking	**nik neraman**	I was taking
hik daramak-n	you are taking	**hik heraman**	you were taking
hark darama	he is taking	**hark zeraman**	he was taking
guk daramagu	we are taking	**guk generaman**	we were taking
zuk daramazu	you are taking	**zuk zeneraman**	you were taking
zuek daramazue	you are taking	**zuek zeneramaten**	you were taking
haiek daramate	they are taking	**haiek zeramaten**	they were taking

GRAMATIK ERREGELAK

"Towards", indicating direction of movement, is translated by the suffix "-arengAnantz" for living beings, and by "-rantz" for inanimate objects. Thus: amarengAnantz, gauzarantz. Their plurals are "-énganantz" and "-etarantz" respectively. Thus: semeenganantz, etxeetarantz.

ARIKETAK

Bainu jantzia ipini nuen eta hondartzara joan nintzen	I put on my bathing suit and went to the beach.
Hondartzako harea bero zegoen	The sand on the beach was hot.
Itsas ertzeko ura hotz dago	The water at the shoreline is cold.
Liburudendako dendariarekin hitz egin dut	I've spoken with the salesgirl at/in the bookstore.
Kafetegian sartu ginen	We entered the cafeteria.
Diruzainak kutxan dirua dauka	The cashier has the money in the box.
Diruzainak dirua du	The cashier has money.
Janaridendan janariak daude	There is food in the grocery store.
Harategian okela dute	They have meat at the butcher's.
Dendako diruzainaren kutxa handia da	The store cashier's box (register) is big.
Diruzaina kutxarantz joan zen	The cashier went towards the cash register.
Aparkalekuetan autoak daude	There are cars in the parking lots.
Aparkaleku hori ez da merke, garesti baizik	That parking lot isn't cheap, but expensive.
Jantziak kendu eta itsasoan sartu ginen	We took off our clothes and went into the sea.
Nola zegoen itsasoko ura?. Beroa	How was the sea water? Warm.
Hibaian arrain asko dago	There are many fish in the river.
Hibaiak itsasorantz doaz	Rivers flow towards the sea.
Zer hartuko duzu?. Kafesnea	What will you have? Coffee with milk.
Nola zaude?. Ongi	How are you? Well/fine.
Dendariak bainu jantzia zeraman	The salesman took the swimming suit.
Zer daramazu?. Ogia. Okela	What are you carrying? Bread. Meat.
Zer daramazue?. Arraina eta esnea	What are you taking? Fish and milk.
Zainduko duzu dendako kutxa?	Will you take care of the cash register in the store?
Ez, ez dut zainduko	No, I won't take care of it.
Dendatik irten zineten	You left the shop.

HAMABOSGARREN IKASGAIA
LESSON FIFTEEN
HIZTEGIA

itzuli	return/go back	**lagun**	companion
		adiskide	friend
izerdi	sweat	**lan**	work (noun)
odol	blood	**lan egin**	work (verb)
jarri	put	**landare**	plant
jezarri, eseri	sit down	**leku, toki**	place
jaun	gentleman	**lur**	earth/land
jo	hit/play an instrument	**madari**	pear
nigar egin	cry	**sagar**	apple
kafesne	coffee with milk	**laranja**	orange
kaiola	cage	**ke**	smoke

ADITZA
NOR NORI*

Indikatibozko orainaldia		**Indikatibozko lehenaldia**	
Hura	it	**Hura**	it
niri ERORI zait	I've dropped it	niri ERORI zitzaidan	I dropped it
hari ERORI zaio	he's dropped it	hari ERORI zitzaion	he dropped it
guri ERORI zaigu	we've dropped it	guri ERORI zitzaigun	we dropped it
zuri ERORI zaizu	you've dropped it	zuri ERORI zitzaizun	you dropped it
zuei ERORI zaizue	you've dropped it	zuei ERORI zitzai-/zuen	you dropped it
haiei ERORI zaie	they've dropped it	haiei ERORI zitzaien	they dropped it

OHARRA.—The main verb, ERORI, has been printed in capital letters. In its place we could put many other main verbs. Thus: niri APURTU zait = It has broken (re: me), etc.

*T.N.: The NOR -NORI conjugation is difficult for the English mentality as it expresses relationships which find no grammatical equivalent in our language. In general, it can be explained thus: verbs of movement, which in English are considered intransitive, can in Basque be seen as having an animate recipient of the action. The person affected by the movement is indicated by the final morpheme of the auxiliary: Osaba etorri zait = My uncle has come (and this affects me; his coming has happened to me).

With transitive verbs such as "drop", "lose", "forget", etc., the use of this conjugation denotes a relationship sometimes called the "dative of interest". The English subject of the verb becomes, in Basque, the recipient of the action; i.e. if I drop, lose or forget my books, their falling, being lost or forgotten affects me. Thus, Liburuak erori (galdu, ahaztu) zaizkit = The books have fallen (been lost or forgotten), and this has happened to me.

Whenever these relationships cannot be adequately expressed in translation, either by resorting to the passive voice or with prepositions, normal English syntax will be used followed by the person affected in parentheses for the first few examples: Osaba etorri zait = My uncle has come (re: me).

ARIKETAK

Ikasgaiak ikasi eta ariketak egin ditugu	We've learned the lessons and done the exercises.
Zer diozu?. Gauza asko diot	What are you saying? I'm saying many things.
Zer diote geltokiez?	What are they saying about the stations?
Goizeko zortzietatik gaueko zazpiak arte	From 8 in the morning until 7 p.m.
Zer esan zenioten aitari?	What did you say to Father?
Osabari ez diogu hori esan	We haven't said that to our uncle.
Herriko kaleetara joan naiz	I've gone (in)to the town streets.
Hiriko espaloietatik ibili naiz	I've walked (along) the city sidewalks.
Igandeetako arratsaldeetan	On Sunday afternoons.
Gaur berandu nator	I'm(coming)late today.
Aitaren etxeko leihoak konponduko ditut	I'll fix the windows in Father's house.
Igandean mendiko etxera joan ginen	On Sunday we went to the (our) mountain house (home).
Mendietako zuhaitzetan berde kolore asko dago	There's a lot of green in the trees of the mountains.
Lehengusuak kalean daude eta gu menditik gatoz	Our cousins are outside in the street (in town) and we are coming from the mountain.
Gaur gu etxean gaude eta zuek ikastolara zoazte	Today we are (staying) at home and you are going to school.
Haik hirian zeuden eta gu ohera gindoazen	They were in the city and we were going to bed.
Zuek etxetik zentozten eta ni herrira nindoan	You were coming from home and was I going to the city.
Etxetik herrirako bide zabalean ikusi zintudan	I saw you on the wide road (which goes) from your house to the town.
Hemen nator bidearen erditik	Here I come along the middle of the road.
Neguaren erdian hotz da	It's cold in the middle of Winter.
Urriaren erdian joango naiz	I'll go in the middle of October.
Autobidetik nire etxera hamar minututako bidea dago	There's a ten minute walk from the highway to my house. (It takes 10 minutes...).
Nor zebilen etxeko atean?	Who was hanging around the door of the house?

HAMASEIGARREN IKASGAIA
LESSON SIXTEEN

HIZTEGIA

geratu	stop	okaran	plum
bihurtu	become/turn into/get	olio	oil
gertatu	happen	ondoan	near/by
mahats	grape	ondoren	after
mahasti	grapevine	ordaindu	pay (verb)
mendi	mountain/country (side)	osatu	complete/finish/fill up
zelai	field	sendatu	cure/get well
soro	orchard	oso	very/completely/quite
mesedez	please	otso	wolf
moldatu	form/mold/fit (verbs)	ozpin	vinegar
musu	kiss (noun)	piztu	turn on/light (verb)
moztu	cut	itzali	turn off/put out
neke	fatigue/difficulty	poz	happiness/pleasure

ADITZA

NOR NORI

Indikatibozko orainaldia		**Indikatibozko lehenaldia**	
Haik	**Them**	**Haik**	**Them**
niri ERORI zaizkit	I've dropped them	niri ERORI zitzaizkidan	I dropped them
hiri ERORI zaizkik-n	you've dropped them	hiri ERORI zitzaizkik-nan	you dropped them
hari ERORI zaizkio	he's dropped them	hari ERORI zitzaizkion	he dropped them
guri ERORI zaizkigu	we've dropped them	guri ERORI zitzaizkigun	we dropped them
zuri ERORI zaizkizu	you've dropped them	zuri ERORI zitzaizkizun	you dropped them
zuei ERORI zaizkizue	you've dropped them	zuei ERORI zitzaizkizuen	you dropped them
haiei ERORI zaizkie	they've dropped them	haiei ERORI zitzaizkien	they dropped them

OHARRA.—Notice the difference between this conjugation and the one in the previous lesson. In Lesson 15, what had fallen or been dropped was singular (it), whereas in this conjugation the verb is pluralized. Thus, I have dropped a pear/a pear has fallen (re: me) = madari bat erori zait; but, I have dropped the apples / the apples have fallen (re: me) = sagarrak erori zaizkit.

ARIKETAK

Orain gogoratu naiz hartaz	I've just now remembered it (that).
Olioaz bigundu zitzaion	With oil, it got softer (for him).
Ahantzi zitzaigun	We forgot it. (it was forgotten by us).
Musu bat eman dio	He's given her a kiss.
Argia itzali zitzaien	The light went off. (re: them).
Odola irten zitzaidan	I was bleeding.
Liburu asko generaman	We were carrying many books.
Sorotik mahatsa nekarren	I was bringing grape(s) from the orchard.
Gutti zenbiltzan alabarekin	You walked very little with your daughter.
Gela hau amarentzat zen	This room was for Mother.
Herrira bide zabaletik gentozen	We took the wide (main) road into town.
Jantokitik sukalderako bidean ikusi zintudan	I saw you on the way from the dining room to the kitchen.
Atezain gaiztoarekin zegoen	He was with the bad doorman.
Atezainarekin ikusi nuen	I saw him with the doorman.
Ekaitza trumoi eta tximistarekin hasi eta euriarekin bukatu zen	The storm began with thunder and lightning and ended with rain.
Osaben semearen etxeko atea	My uncles' son's house door.
Ahaide zaharren semeen herria	(Our) ancestors' sons' town.
Etxeko gela batetan daukat	I have it in a room of the house.
Hori bezalako gauzarik ez dut ikusi	I've never seen anything like that/it.
Ez dut osabarik ez izebarik	I have neither uncles nor aunts.
Ez genekien gauza askorik	We didn't know many things.
Nortzu etorri ziren atzo arratsaldean?	Who came yesterday afternoon?
Gaur goizeko euria handia izan da	The rain this morning (this morning's rain) has been very heavy.
Iraileko hogeitik abenduko hamaikararte	From the 20th of September until December 11th.
Goizetik eguerdiko ordu batak arte	From morning until 1 p.m.
Herriko kaleak ibili nituen	I walked the streets of the town.
Etxeek gelak dituzte	Houses have rooms.
Herrira zatozte. Ez zoazte hirira	You're coming to the town . You're not going to the city.
Mendirantz zindoazten	You were going towards the mountain.
Neguan ez gindoazen mendira	We didn't go to the mountain in Winter.
Etxetik hirira gentozen	We were coming from home to the city.

HAMAZAZPIGARREN IKASGAIA
LESSON SEVENTEEN

HIZTEGIA

poxpolu	match (noun)	maite ukan, maitatu	love (verb)
praka	pants	telebista	television
prestatu	prepare/get ready	irrati	radio
sabel	abdomen	teilatu	roof
sagardo	cider	untzi	boat/ship
gari	wheat	urdaiazpiko	ham
garagardo	beer	uso	dove
garagar	barley	uste	opinion/belief
salda	broth	txartel	ticket
sarrera	entrance	txakur	dog
sendo	strong	katu	cat
soldata	wage (noun)	zapi	cloth
su	fire/flame	zarata	noise
entzun	hear	zati	piece/bit
		zebrabide	crosswalk

ADITZA

ZER NORK

Indikatibozko orainaldia		Indikatibozko lehenaldia	
Ni	**me**	**Ni**	**me**
hark IKUSI nau	he has seen me	hark IKUSI ninduen	he saw me
zuk IKUSI nauzu	you have seen me	zuk IKUSI ninduzun	you saw me
zuek IKUSI nauzue	you have seen me	zuek IKUSI ninduzuen	you saw me
haiek IKUSI naute	they have seen me	haiek IKUSI ninduten	they saw me

OHARRA.—The main verb is in capital letters. In its place we could put any of the other transitive verbs. Thus: ERAMAN ninduen = he took me, ATXILOTU naute = they have arrested me, HARTU nauzue = you've caught me.

ARIKETAK

Poxpoluak erori zaizkizu	You've dropped the matches.
Gaur goizean ikusi zaitut	I've seen you this morning.
Ikusi ninduzun atzo?	Did you see me yesterday?
Ez, atzo ez ninduzun ikusi	No, yesterday you didn't see me.
Atzo ikusi ninduzun	You saw me yesterday.
Sagarrak ez zaizkizu erori	You haven't dropped the apples.
Sagarrak erori zaizkizu	You've dropped the apples.
Erori zaizkizu sagarrak?	Have you dropped the apples?
Erori al zaizkizu sagarrak?	Have you dropped the apples?
Etorri da?. Etorri al da?	Has he come? Has he come?
Gizon haiek sagardoa erosi zidaten	Those men bought me the cider.
Entzun ninduzun irratitik?	Did you hear me on the radio?
Poxpolua itzali zitzaidan	The match went out (on me).
Zu ikusteak poztu nau	To see you has made me happy.
Tristatu nauzu	You've made me sad.
Maite nauzu?. Ez nauzu maite	Do you love me? You don't love me.
Zure ondoan nauzu	You have me at your side.
Entzun ninduzun?. Ez ninduzun entzun	Did you hear me? You didn't hear me.
Entzun ninduzun	You heard me.
Kaletik txakurrarekin ikusi naute	They have seen me in the street with the dog.
Urdaiazpikoa erori zitzaidan	I dropped the ham.
Oso zikin utzi nauzu	You got me all dirty.
Ile beltzak zuri bihurtu zaizkit	My black hair has turned white.

Nire anaiari prakak zikindu zitzaizkion	My brother's pants got dirty.
Zarata asko zegoen eta ez ninduzun entzun	There was a lot of noise and you didn't hear me.

HAMAZORTZIGARREN IKASGAIA
LESSON EIGHTEEN

HIZTEGIA

zerbitzari	one who serves	**agertu**	appear
zerbitzatu	serve	**agindu**	give orders
zerbitzu	service	**agintari**	person who gives orders
zubi	bridge	**menpeko**	subordinate
erle	bee	**agiri**	evident
ezti	honey	**aipatu**	mention
maitasun	love (noun)	**aitortu**	confess
gorroto	hatred	**behar**	must/going to/intend to
gorrotatu	hate (verb)	**akats**	defect
abiatu	start off/get going	**ukitu**	touch (on)
		alargun -tsa	widower/widow
adierazi	give the impression	**aldapa**	slope
aditu	understand	**aldare**	altar
beste	other/another	**alde**	for/on the side of
zerbait	something	**alde egin, aldendu**	go away, out
gai	subject/theme		
alderdi	(political) party		
nekatu	get tired	**talde**	group

ADITZA

ZER NORK

Indikatibozko orainaldia		Indikatibozko lehenaldia	
Gu	us	**Gu**	us
hark IKUSI gaitu	he has seen us	**hark IKUSI gintuen**	he saw us
zuk IKUSI gaituzu	you have seen us	**zuk IKUSI gintuzun**	you saw us
zuek IKUSI gaituzue	you have seen us	**zuek IKUSI gintuzuen**	you saw us
haiek IKUSI gaitue	they have seen us	**haiek IKUSI gintuzten**	they saw us

GRAMATIK ERREGELAK

In order to indicate that we are speaking **about** something, the suffix "-az" is added to the noun in the singular and "-ez" to the noun in the plural. Thus: **Gizonaz hitz egingo dugu** = we shall speak about the man, **mendiez hitz egin genuen** = we spoke about the mountains; **mendiez hitz egin dugu** = we have spoken about the mountains. However, we are (now) speaking = **hitz egiten ari gara**, must be kept distinct from the present (habitual) **hitz egiten dugu** = we speak. (See note, Lesson Twelve). In both of these present tenses, the addition of the suffix "-ten" to the verb indicates continuous action, but the choice of auxiliary is what gives us a precise idea of tense. Thus: **jaten ari naiz** = I am eating, **edaten ari gara** = we are drinking.

ARIKETAK

Aurpegia garbitzen ari naiz	I am washing my face.
Janzten ari nintzen	I was getting dressed.
Atzo gauean dantzan egin genuen	We danced last ninght.
Zertaz hitz egin duzue?	What have you talked about?
Politikaz ari ginen	We were (talking) about politics.
Alderdi politikoez ari zineten?	About political parties?
Ez, taldeez	No, about groups.
Zer aipatu duzue?	What have you mentioned?
Maitasuna eta gorrotoa aipatu ditugu	We've mentioned love and hate.
Eta zer gehiago?	And what else (more)?
Aitortu behar dut beste zerbait	I must confess something else.
Beste gai batzu ukitu ditugu	We've touched on other subjects.
Adibidez, aberastasuna eta pobretasuna	For example, wealth and poverty.
Gauza agiria da, agintariak agintzen du	It's obvious (an obvious thing) that the authorities give orders.
Eta menpekoak obeditzen du	And the subordinate obeys.
Akats asko dago	There are many defects.
Aldapa gora nekatu egin ginen	We got tired (going) up the slope.
Nor ari da gorrotatzen?	Who hates? (lit. who is hating?).
Idazten ari dira. Irakurtzen ari da	They are writing. He is reading.
Ikusten gaitu. Pozten naute	He sees us. They make me happy.
Erortzen zaizkit. Apurtzen zizaizkion	I drop them. They broke (re: him).
Gizonaren alde dago	He's on the man's side.
Gizonaren alde egin du	He's done (something) in the man's favor.
Iñaki, etxean al dago?	Is Iñaki at home?
·Ez, alde egin du	No, he's gone out/away.

HEMERETZIGARREN IKASGAIA
LESSON NINETEEN

HIZTEGIA

bizkor	agile/quick	**aurkitu**	find/discover
alfer	lazy	**arrantzale**	fisherman
elkar	each other/together	**arrantzatu**	fish (verb)
elkarrizketa	(have a) conversation	**arrazoi**	reason
amildu	collapse	**arren**	please
		arrisku	risk (noun)
erori	fall/down, out	**arriskatu**	(run a) risk
altxatu	get up	**amore eman**	concede/give in
antz	likeness		

ADITZA

ZER NORK

Indikatibozko orainaldia		**Indikatibozko lehenaldia**	
Zu you (sing.)		**Zu** you (sing.)	
nik IKUSI zaitut	I have seen you	nik IKUSI zintudan	I saw you
hark IKUSI zaitu	He has seen you	hark IKUSI zintuen	He saw you
guk IKUSI zaitugu	We have seen you	guk IKUSI zintugun	We saw you
haiek IKUSI zaituzte	They have seen you	haiek IKUSI zintuzten	They saw you
Zuek you (pl.)		**Zuek** you (pl.)	
nik IKUSI zaituztet	I have seen you	nik IKUSI zintuztedan	I saw you
hark IKUSI zaituzte	He has seen you	hark IKUSI zintuzten	He saw you
guk IKUSI zaituztegu	We have seen you	guk IKUSI zintuztegun	We saw you
haiek IKUSI zaituztete	They have seen you	haiek IKUSI zintuzteten	They saw you

GRAMATIK ERREGELAK

The English preposition "from" is indicated in Basque by the suffix "-ARENGANDIK" for living beings and by "-TIK" for inanimate objects. Their respective plurals are "-ENGANDIK" and "-ETATIK". Thus: **amarengandik datorren maitasuna** = the love that comes from the mother, **gizonengandik sortzen diren problemak** = the problems which arise from men, **hiritik datorren bidea** = the road that comes from the city, **mendietatik jaisten diren urak** = the waters which come down from the mountains.

"To" (direction of movement) is indicated by "-ARENGANA" for living beings in the singular, and by "-RA" for inanimate objects in the singular. Their respective plurals are "-ENGANA" and "-ETARA".

"To/up to" (with the idea of arriving at) is indicated by "-ARENGANAINO" for living beings and by "-RAINO" for inanimate objects. Their plurals are "-ENGANAINO" and "-ETARAINO".

"Towards" is indicated by "-ARENGANANTZ" for living beings and by "-RANTZ" for inanimate objects. Plurals: "-ENGANANTZ" and "-ETARANTZ".

ARIKETAK

Gaur hartuko dugu Bilbotik Donostiraino doan autobidea	Today we'll take the highway which goes from Bilbao to San Sebastian.
Iruinera joan zarete?	Have you been to Pamplona?
Ez, Gasteizera joan gara	No, we've been to Vitoria.
Gazte horrek amarenganako maitasun handia du	That boy feels great love for his mother.
Artzainenganantz joan ginen	We went towards the shepherds.
Herriraino joan gara	We've gone to (and arrived at) the town.
Lehengusinaren etxeraino joan ginen	We went as far as our cousin's house.
Aitonarengana etorri ziren	They came to (where) Grandfather (was).
Etxe hori amonarengatik erosi genuen	We bought that house because of Grandmother
Etxera etorri zitzaigun	He came to our house. (re: us).
Arraina arrantzalearenganantz zihoan	The fish was going towards the fisherman.
Elkarrizketan ikusi zintuzten	They saw you having a conversation.
Gora altxatu zintuztegun	We lifted you up.
Elizako aldarean ikusi zintuzten	They saw you at the church altar.
Atzo goizean herrian ikuzi zintudan	I saw you in town yesterday morning.

HOGEIGARREN IKASGAIA — LESSON TWENTY

HIZTEGIA

harro	proud	**sehaska**	cradle
apal	humble	**aski**	enough
arrotz	foreigner	**asmatu**	invent/make up
arrunt	current	**aspaldi**	a while/long time ago
arte	until/between	**bururatu**	occur to/think up, of
arto	corn	**aspertu**	be, get bored
artaburu	cob	**asto**	burro
hartz	bear (noun)	**atertu**	clear up
asaldatu	confront	**hats**	breath
ase izan	be full (re: eating)		

ADITZA

ZER NORI NORK

Indikatibozko orainaldia

Hura   it

nik hari **EMAN diot**   I've given it to him
nik zuri **EMAN dizut** I've given it to you

nik zuei **EMAN dizuet** I've given it to you
nik haiei **EMAN diet**   I've given it to them

Haik   them

nik hari **EMAN dizkiot**   I've given them to him
nik zuri **EMAN dizkizut** I've given them to you

nik zuei **EMAN dizkizuet** I've given them to you
nik haiei **EMAN dizkiet**   I've given them to them

Indikatibozko lehenaldia

Hura   it

nik hari **EMAN nion**   I gave it to him
nik zuri **EMAN nizun**   I gave it to you

nik zuei **EMAN nizuen** I gave it to you
nik haiei **EMAN nien**   I gave it to them

Haik   them

nik hari **EMAN nizkion** I gave them to him
nik zuri **EMAN nizkizun** I gave them to you

nik zuei **EMAN nizkizuen** I gave them to you
nik haiei **EMAN nizkien**   I gave them to them

OHARRA.—Observe that in these conjugations different forms are used for singular and plural direct objects; that is, the verb is singular or pluralized according to whether we are "giving" ONE thing or SEVERAL. Thus: asto bat eman dizut = I've given you a burro, astoak eman dizkizut = I've given you the burros.

42

GRAMATIK ERREGELAK

COMPARATIVES.– "Hain" in Basque means "so/such a". Thus: It's such a beautiful mountain! = **mendia hain ederra da!** Why are you going so quickly? = **zergatik zoaz hain arin?**

"As... as" in Basque is "bezain". Thus: **Hibai hori ez da hau bezain zabala** = that river isn't as wide as this one.

"So much/many" in Basque is "hainbeste". Thus: **zergatik egin duzu hainbeste lan?** = Why have you done so much work?

"As much/many ...as" in Basque is "beste". Thus: As many men as women have come = **gizon beste andre etorri dira.**

ARIKETAK

Zergatik zara hain harro?	Why are you so proud?
Ez naiz harroa, apala baizik	I'm not proud, but humble.
Hori ez dizut sinesten	I don't believe that (of you).
Bihar sagarrak erosiko dizkizut	Tomorrow I'll buy you apples.
Atzo praka berri batzu erosi nizkion	Yesterday I bought him some new pants.
Hainbat gauza erosi dizuet	I've bought you (so) many things.
Liburu hori ihaz eman nizun	I gave you that book last year.
Aspaldi ekarri nizkien	I brought them for them a long time ago.
Zer bururatu zaizu?	What has occured to you?
Gauza on bat bururatu zait	Something good has occured to me.
Euria da. Gero atertuko da	It's raining. Later it will clear up.
Zer esan didazu?	What did you say to me?
Ez dizut ongi ulertu. Esan berriz	I haven't understood you well. Say it again.
Ez nituen hirian ikusi	I didn't see them in town.
Arrantzalea ikusi dut	I've seen the fisherman.
Elkarrizketan ikusi nituen	I saw them talking together.

HOGEITABATGARREN IKASGAIA
LESSON TWENTY-ONE

HIZTEGIA

bakar bat	only one	**non**	where
bakartate	solitude	**nonahi**	anywhere
bakarrik	alone	**nonbait**	somewhere
norbait	someone	**edonon**	wherever
nornahi	anyone	**nola, zelan**	how/what... like?/how come?
edonor	whoever	**edonola, edozelan**	anyhow/anyway
zerbait	something	**inon**	anywhere/nowhere
zernahi	anything	**inoiz**	ever/never
edozer	whatever	**inor**	anyone/no one
noiz	when		
noiznahi	anytime		
noizbait	sometime		
edonoiz	whenever/always		

ADITZA

ZER NORI NORK

Indikatibozko orainaldia

Hura	it
hark niri EMAN dit	He has given it to me
hark hari EMAN dio	He has given it to him
hark guri EMAN digu	He has given it to us
hark zuri EMAN dizu	He has given it to you
hark zuei EMAN dizue	He has given it to you
hark haiei EMAN die	He has given it to them

Indikatibozko orainaldia

Haik	them
hark niri EMAN dizkit	He has given them to me
hark hari EMAN dizkio	He has given them to him
hark guri EMAN dizkigu	He has given them to us
hark zuri EMAN dizkizu	He has given them to you
hark zuei EMAN dizkizue	He has given them to you
hark haiei EMAN dizkie	He has given them to them

GRAMATIK ERREGELAK

A subordinate clause is indicated in Basque by adding the suffix "-(E)LA" (remember that A+E=E) to the verb. Thus: **ni naiz** = I am; ...that I am = **ni naizela, hura da** = he is, ...that he is = **hura dela**. There exist a few exceptions in which only "-LA" is added: **doa** = he is going, **doala** = ...that he is going. **Ikusi dut** becomes **ikusi dudala** = ...that I've seen it.

Subordinate clauses which in English are introduced by "because/due to" (i.e. which tell us "why" something has happened) are indicated by adding the suffix "-(E)LAKO" to the clausal verb. Thus: **etorri da** = he has come; **etorri delako** = ...because he has come; **egin du** = he has done it, **egin duelako** = ...because he has done it/that.

"Why?" in Basque is "zergatik". Thus: why have you done that? = **Zergatik egin duzu hori?**

Clauses which in English are introduced by "since/as (because)" in Basque are introduced by "zeren" with the word "bait" placed just before the auxiliary verb in the clause in question. "Bait" becomes a prefix of this auxiliary verb, causing the following changes in spelling: **T+G = K, T+D = T, T+N = N, T+L = L.** Thus:

Since I've come = **zeren etorri bait + naiz = zeren etorri bainaiz**
Since I have it = **zeren bait + dut = zeren baitut**
Since we are = **zeren bait + gara = zeren baikara**
Since he was = **zeren bait + zegoen = zeren baitzegoen**

ARIKETAK

Zergatik apurtu duzue liburu hori?	Why have you broken that book?
Liburu hori, atsegin ez dugulako apurtu dugu	We've broken that book because we don't like it.
Zergatik etorri zarete hain arin?	Why have you come so quickly?
Zuekin egon nahi genuelako etorri gara hain arin	We've come so quickly because we wanted to be with you.
Zergatik zaude bakarrik?	Why are you alone?
Bakartatea atsegin dudalako nago bakarrik	I'm alone because I like being alone. (solitude).
Haurra lotan dago. Loak hartu du	The child is sleeping. He's fallen asleep.
Edozer gauza egingo nuke hori lortzeagatik	I'd do anything to get that.
Noiz joango naiz zure etxera?	When will I go to your house?
Etor noiznahi	Come whenever you want/anytime.
Geuk ditugu, zeren hark eman baitizkigu	We've got them because he gave them to us.
Hark eman dizkigulako ditugu guk	We've got them because he gave them to us.

HOGEITABIGARREN IKASGAIA
LESSON TWENTY-TWO

HIZTEGIA

atsekabe	hurt (noun)	aza	cabbage
atso	old person	azal	bark/peel/envelope
agure	old person		
atxakia	pretext/excuse	posta	mail
ahul	weak	postari	mailman
ahuntz	goat	azeri	fox
aurten	this year	azpi	below/under(neath)/lower
ausart	daring	azpimarkatu	underline
hauts	ash	gain	above/upper
hauzi	lawsuit/matter	azpijan	undermine
hauzitegi	law court		
axola	worry/care	baina	but
ez dit axola	I don't care		

ADITZA

ZER NORI NORK

Indikatibozko lehenaldia		Indikatibozko lehenaldia	
Hura	**it**	**Haik**	**them**
hark niri EMAN zidan	he gave it to me	hark niri EMAN zizkidan	he gave them to me
hark hari EMAN zion	he gave it to him	hark hari EMAN zizkion	he gave them to him
hark guri EMAN zigun	he gave it to us	hark guri EMAN zizkigun	he gave them to us
hark zuri EMAN zizun	he gave it to you	hark zuri EMAN zizkizun	he gave them to you
hark zuei EMAN zizuen	he gave it to you	hark zuei EMAN zizkizuen	he gave them to you
hark haiei EMAN zien	he gave it to them	hark haiei EMAN zizkien	he gave them to them

GRAMATIK ERREGELAK

COMPARATIVES.– Continuing with the comparatives, "more than" is "baino gehiago", "less than" is "baino gutiago", etc. Examples:

greater/more than = **baino handiago**
smaller/less than = **baino tikiago**
dirtier than = **baino lohiago**
cleaner than = **baino garbiago**

ARIKETAK

Hemen gaude, zeren etorri baikara	Here we are, since we've come.
Etorri garelako gaude hemen	We are here because we have come.
Nola zaude? Ongi, eta zu?. Ni ere ongi	How are you? Fine, and you? I'm fine too.
Nola egin duzu lo?. Ongi, eta zuk?. Nik ere ongi	How have you slept? Well, and you? Me too.
Hor norbait dago. Bai, norbait dago hor	Someone is there. Yes, there is someone there.
Gizon bakar bat ere ez da etorri	Not even one man has come.
Ikastolan liburuak eman dizkidate	They've given me books at school.
Amari poxpoluak erosi behar dizkiot	I have to buy mother some matches.
Zer esan dizu gizon horrek?. Ezer ez	What has that man told you? Nothing.
Inor etorri al da?. Ez, inor ez	Has anyone come? No, no one.
Postariak eskutitz bat ekarri zion	The mailman brought him a letter.
Seiluak kanpokoak zituen	It had stamps from abroad.
Gaina azpia baino gorago dago	The upper (part) is higher than the lower.
Aurten ihaz baino hotz gehiago egin du	This year has been colder than last.
Ahuntzek azak jan zituzten	The goats ate the cabbages.
Atxakia batzu eman zizkidan	He gave me some excuses.
Hauzitegira eraman gintuzten	They took us to court (the courts).
Hori azpimarkatu zigun	He underlined that for us.
Bost axola zaizkit	I don't care at all.
Laranjak eraman zizkizuen	They took you (some) oranges.
Etxea erori zitzaien	Their house collapsed.

HOGEITAHIRUGARREN IKASGAIA
LESSON TWENTY-THREE

HIZTEGIA

baizik	but (rather)	**batasun**	unity/unification
bake	peace		
gerra	war	**bazter**	corner
gudukatu	fight (verb)	**bedeinkatu**	bless
bakoitz	each	**madarikatu**	condemn/repudiate
balea	whale		
ba-	if (conditional)	**behin**	once
baliatu	use/base something on	**behintzat**	at least
barkatu	forgive	**bekoki, kopeta**	forehead
bart	last night	**belaun**	knee
batu	unify/unite	**eskerrak**	thanks

ADITZA

ZER NORI NORK

Indikatibozko orainaldia **Indikatibozko lehenaldia**

Hura	**it**	**Hura**	**it**
guk hari EMAN diogu	we've given it to him	**guk hari EMAN genion**	we gave it to him
guk zuri EMAN dizugu	we've given it to you	**guk zuri EMAN genizun**	we gave it to you
guk zuei EMAN dizuegu	we've given it to you	**guk zuei EMAN genizuen**	we gave it to you
guk haiei EMAN diegu	we've given it to them	**guk haiei EMAN genien**	we gave it to them

Haik	**them**	**Haik**	**them**
guk hari EMAN dizkiogu	we've given them to him	**guk hari EMAN genizkion**	we gave them to him
guk zuri EMAN dizkizugu	we've given them to you	**guk zuri EMAN genizkizun**	we gave them to you
guk zuei EMAN dizkizuegu	we've given them to you	**guk zuei EMAN genizki-/zuen**	we gave them to you
guk haiei EMAN dizkiegu	we've given them to them	**guk haiei EMAN genizkien**	we gave them to them

GRAMATIK ERREGELAK

In previous lessons we have seen the prepositions in connection with animate and inanimate (noun) objects. Now we shall examine them in connection with noun objects which in Basque are considered to be "indefinite". Proper names, nouns qualified by numbers or adverbs of quantity, and nouns considered generically (see Note, Lesson One, Gramatik Erregelak) do not take an article. (T.N.: Since both the articles and prepositions are indicated by suffixes, the prepositional suffix is somewhat different when the noun in seen as "indefinite" and therefore admits no article. For further explanations on prepositions, see Gramatik Erregelak, Lessons 8-12, 18, 19).

The subject of a transitive verb ends in "-K" when preceded by a vowel, and in "-EK" when preceded by a consonant.
Hainbat gizonek egin dute = many men have done it
Hainbat gizon etorri da = many men have come
"To/at" (see Lesson 9 and T.N. Lesson 15) are indicated by the suffix "-RI" (following a vowel) and "-I" after a consonant:
Gizon askori ez zaio hori gustatzen = that isn't pleasing to many men (many men don't like that).
Observe that the verb is conjugated both in singular and plural with these "indefinite" forms.
Possession (see Lesson 10) is indicated by "-REN" after a vowel and by "-EN" after a consonant:
Lau andreren eta bost gizonen etxeak = the houses of 4 women and 5 men.

ARIKETAK

Gauza asko erosi zizkien	They bought them many things.
Loreak etxe ondoan ipini zizkion	He put the flowers near the house.
Etxea egiteko harea ekarri zigun	He brought us sand to make the house.
Olioagatik guti ordaindu zion, baina bihar gehiago emango dio	He paid him little for the oil, but tomorrow he'll give him more.
Zer ekarri zizuen?. Ez zizuen ezer ekarri	What did they bring you? They didn't bring you anything.
Gizon bakoitzak du bere problema	Each man has his own problem.
Gizonek gerla egin zuten	Men made (waged) war.
Gizonek gudukatu ziren	Men fought.
Hainbat gizon gudukatu zen	Many men fought.
Eskerrak eman genizkion	We thanked him. (We gave him our thanks).
Eskerrik asko. Ez da zergatik. Milesker	Thanks very much. You're welcome. A thousand thanks.
Arrainak biharko eman dizkizuegu	We've given you the fish for tomorrow.
Aranak ekarri genizkizun. Jan al dituzu?	We brought you the plums. Have you eaten them?
Kafesnea ekarri genizun, baina zuk ez zenuen hartu nahi izan	We brought you coffee with milk, but you didn't wish to drink it.
Bost gizoni deitu diet hori egiteko	I've called five men to do that.

HOGEITALAUGARREN IKASGAIA
LESSON TWENTY-FOUR

HIZTEGIA

beldur	fear		beti	always
bele	crow		batzutan	sometimes
berandu	late		gehiegitan	too often
beraz	so/thus/therefore		gutitan	seldom
berdin	same/equal		sarri	frequently
berehala	right away		sarri askotan	many times
besarkatu	embrace		sarri asko	very often
bete	full		bezpera	eve/night before
bete ukan	fill		jai	holiday/festival
ikaratu	frighten		astegun	work day
txanpon	coin		jaiegun	holiday/day off

ADITZA

ZER NORI NORK

Indikatibozko orainaldia

Hura   it

zuk niri EMAN **didazu** you've given it to me
zuk hari EMAN **diozu** you've given it to him
zuk guri EMAN **diguzu** you've given it to us
zuk haiei EMAN **diezu** you've given it to them

Haik   them

zuk niri EMAN **dizkidazu** you've given them to me
zuk hari EMAN **dizkiozu** you've given them to him
zuk guri EMAN **dizkiguzu** you've given them to us
zuk haiei EMAN **dizkiezu** you've given them to them

Indikatibozko lehenaldia

Hura   it

zuk niri EMAN **zenidan** you gave it to me
zuk hari EMAN **zenion** you gave it to him
zuk guri EMAN **zenigun** you gave it to us
zuk haiei EMAN **zenien** you gave it to them

Haik   them

zuk niri EMAN **zenizkidan** you gave them to me
zuk hari EMAN **zenizkion** you gave them to him
zuk guri EMAN **zenizkigun** you gave them to us
zuk haiei EMAN **zenizkien** you gave them to them

GRAMATIK ERREGELAK

We shall continue with prepositions taking "indefinite" objects. "For" (see Lesson twelve) is indicated by "-RENTZAT" following a vowel and by "-ENTZAT" after a consonant:

Hau gizonentzat da = that is for men

"With" is indicated by "-REKIN" after a vowel and by "EKIN" after a consonant:

Gizon askorekin hitz egin zuen = he spoke with many men

"About/by" (see Lesson 18) is indicated by "-Z" and "-EZ":

Mendiz eta oihanez hitz egin zuten = they talked about mountains and forests

"In/on/during etc." (see Lesson 11) is indicated by "-TAN" and "-ETAN":

Menditan eta oihanetan = in mountains and forests

ARIKETAK

Inoiz joan al zara hirira?. Ez, inoiz ez	Have you ever been to town? No, never.
Soldatak ordaindu dizkigute	They paid us (our) wages.
Barkatu du. Ez du barkatu. Barkatu al du?	He's forgiven her. He hasn't forgiven her. Has he forgiven her?
Madarikatu du. Madarikatu egin du	He has damned (cursed) him.
Euskararen batasuna eskatu dizuegu	We've asked you for the unification of the Basque language.
Gauza asko esan dizugu	We've told you many things.
Gauzak esan dizkizugu	We've told you things.
Zer esan genion?. Ezer ez	What did we say to him? Nothing.
Beldur naiz ilunetan	I'm afraid of (in) the dark.
Atzo liburuak ekarri zizkidaten	Yesterday they brought me books.
Zergatik ez zenizkidan ekarri paperak?	Why didn't you bring me the papers?
Ez nizkizun ekarri berandu egin zelako	I didn't bring them because it got late.
Asteak sei astegun eta jaiegun bat ditu	The week has six work days and one holiday.
Beldur eman didazu	You've frightened me (...given me fear).
Beleak ikaratu zion	The crow frightened her.
Berdin zait. Ez zait berdin. Berdin al zaizu?	I don't care (It's the same to me). It isn't the same to me. Do you care?
Etorri zen, beraz, hemen zegoen	He came, so he was here.

HOGEITABOSGARREN IKASGAIA
LESSON TWENTY-FIVE

HIZTEGIA

bidali	send	**biribil**	round
bider, aldiz	time	**biriki**	lung
bildots	lamb	**birjina**	virgin
bildu	collect/gather/pick (up)	**birtute**	virtue
bilduma	collection	**bitarte**	intermediate
biluzik	nude	**bitxi**	jewelry (piece of) / curious
bihotz	heart	**bihurri**	naughty
birao	blasphemy	**bizkar**	back/shoulder

ADITZA

ZER NORI NORK

Indikatibozko orainaldia

Hura   it

zuek niri **EMAN didazue** you've given it to me
zuek hari **EMAN diozue** you've given it to him
zuek guri **EMAN diguzue** you've given it to us
zuek haiei **EMAN diezue** you've given it to them

Haik   them

zuek niri **EMAN dizkidazue** you've given them to me

zuek hari **EMAN dizkiozue** you've given them to him

zuek guri **EMAN dizkiguzue** you've given them to us

zuek haiei **EMAN dizkiezue** you've given them to them

Indikatibozko lehenaldia

Hura   it

zuek niri **EMAN zenidaten** you gave it to me
zuek hari **EMAN zenioten** you gave it to him
zuek guri **EMAN zeniguten** you gave it to us
zuek haiei **EMAN zenieten** you gave it to them

Haik   them

zuek niri **EMAN zenizkida-/ten** you gave them to me

zuek hari **EMAN zenizkio-/ten** you gave them to him

zuek guri **EMAN zenizki-/guten** you gave them to us

zuek haiei **EMAN zenizkie-/ten** you gave them to them

GRAMATIK ERREGELAK

Prepositions taking "indefinite" objects: "From" (See Lesson 19) is indicated by "-TATIK" and by "-ETATIK":

herri askotatik etorri ziren = they came from many towns

"To" (See Lesson 19) is indicated by "-TARA" and by "-ETARA":

mendi askotara igon ginen = we climbed (to) many mountains

"From/of/in etc." (See Lesson 12) is indicated by "-TAKO" and "-ETAKO":

bi Estatutako armadak burrukatu ziren = the armies of two nations fought

ARIKETAK

Beti eman dizkidazu goikoak	You've always given me the upper ones.
Ez dizkidazu beti behekoak eman	You haven't always given me the lower ones.
Berehala joango naiz	I'll go right away.
Bost etxetan. Etxeetan	In five houses. In the houses.
Gehiegitan esan didazu hori	You've told me that too many times.
Ordaindu al genion soldata?	Did we pay him (his) wage?
Txartelak eman nizkizun eta txanponak eman zenizkidan	I gave you the tickets and you gave me the coins.
Dendariak madariak eman zizkigun eta guk ordaindu genion	The shopkeeper gave us the apples and we paid him.
Bildots bat bidali zenidaten	You sent me a lamb.
Seiluak bildu ditut, zeren bilduma egiten baitut	I collect stamps since I'm making a collection.
Birikietan min dut	I have pain in (my) lungs.
Atsegin duzu biluzia?	Do you like nudism?
Ohera joateko biluztu egin zen	He got undressed to go to bed.
Eskerrak emango dizkidazue	You'll thank me.
Ez zenizkioten eskerrak eman	You didn't thank him.
Zergatik eman behar dizkizut eskerrak?	Why do I have to thank you?
Gauza bitxiak esan zenizkiguten	You told us curious things.

HOGEITASEIGARREN IKASGAIA
LESSON TWENTY-SIX
HIZTEGIA

hau	he/she/it/this (intr.)		hauk	they/these (intr.)
hori	he/she/it/that (intr.)		horik	they/those (intr.)
* hura	he/she/it/that (intr.)		haik	they/those (intr.)
honek	he/she/it/this (trans.)		hauek	they/these (trans.)
horrek	he/she/it/that (trans.)		horiek	they/those (trans.)
*: hark	he/she/it/that (trans.)		haiek	they/those (trans.)
honi	(to) him/her/it/this		hauei	(to) them/these
horri	(to) him/her/it/that		horiei	(to) them/those
** hari	(to) him/her/it/that		haiei	(to) them/those

* See T.N., Lesson two.
** See Gramatik Erregelak, Lesson nine.

ADITZA

ZER NORI NORK

Inperatiboa

1. NIRI — **1. (TO) ME**

EMAN biezat	he must give me
EMAN iezadazu	you must give me
EMAN biezadate	they must give me

2. HARI — **2. (TO) HIM/HER/IT**

EMAN biezaio	he must give him
EMAN iezaiozu	you must give him
EMAN biezaiote	they must give him

3. GURI — **3. (TO) US**

EMAN biezagu	he must give us
EMAN iezaguzu	you must give us
EMAN iezaguzue	you must give us
EMAN biezagute	they must give us

4. ZURI — **4. (TO) YOU (sing.)**

EMAN biezazu	he must give you
EMAN biezazute	they must give you

5. ZUEI — **5. (TO) YOU (Pl.)**

EMAN biezazue	he must give you
EMAN biezazuete	they must give you

6. HAIEI — **6. (TO) THEM**

EMAN biezaie	he must give them
EMAN iezaiezu	you must give them
EMAN iezaiezue	you must give them
EMAN biezaiete	they must give them

OHARRA.—These forms are used when only one object is "given" (singular direct object). If more than one thing is "given", the letters ZKI are placed directly behind the letters IEZA. Thus: biezazkit, iezazkidazu, etc.

GRAMATIK ERREGELAK

In order to emphasize a certain word in an affirmative sentence, this word is placed immeditely before the verb. Thus:

aitak txakurra ekarri du = txakurra ekarri du aitak = Father has brought the dog (the dog is what Father has brought). In both of the sentences in Basque, the emphasis is on "the dog".

txakurra aitak ekarri du = aitak ekarri du txakurra = Father has brought the dog (Father is the one who has brought the dog). The emphasis is on "Father".

In conjugating verbs in the imperative, conditional and subjunctive, the main verb undergoes certain modifications:

If the verb ends in TU-DU, these final letters are dropped: **apurtu ≈ apur; saldu ≈ sal.**
If the verb ends in **SI, TSI, ZI, TZI, LI, NI**, the letter "i" is dropped: **hasi ≈ has.**
The verb now shows no tense and is "non-finite".

ARIKETAK

Eman iezaiozu txori hori mutil hari	Give that bird to that boy over there.
Ekar biezaio gazte horrek ogia amari	That boy must bring the bread to his mother.
Egin iezaiozue fitxa irakasleari	Do the exercise for the teacher.
Eraman iezaiezue liburua gazte horiei	Take the book to those boys.
Eraman iezaizkiozue liburuak amari	Take mother the books.
Har iezaguzu han goian dagoen kutxa hori	Get us that box which is up there.
Ordain biezaiote berea	They must pay him what's his.
Esan iezadazu berriz	Tell me that again.
Esan iezaiozu zure anaiari hemen nagoela	Tell your brother I'm here.
Jar iezaiozu txapela buru gainean	Put his beret on his head.
Bihar laranjak ekarri behar dizkiguzue	Tomorrow you must bring us the oranges.
Era askotako loreak ekarri zizkiguten	They brought us flowers of many kinds.
Gazte baldar hura ikusi nuen bart	Last night I saw that naughty (bad) boy.
Bihotz oneko andrea da hori	That is a woman of good heart.
Bizkar zabalak ditu	He has wide shoulders.
Bitxi ederrak erosi dizkidazue	You've brought me beautiful jewelry.
Ogi biribil bat bidali zenidaten	You sent me a round (loaf of) bread.
Birtute handiko andrea da	She is a woman of great virtue.

HOGEITAZAZPIGARREN IKASGAIA
LESSON TWENTY-SEVEN

HIZTEGIA

honen	this one's	**hauen**	their/of these
horren	that one's	**horien**	their/of those
haren	that one's his/its	**haien**	their/of those
honentzat	for this one	**hauentzat**	for them/these
horrentzat	for that one	**horientzat**	for them/those
harentzat	for that one	**haientzat**	for them/those
honegatik	because of this	**hauengatik**	because of them/these
horregatik	because of that	**horiengatik**	because of them/those
honekin	because of that	**hauekin**	because of them/those
horrekin	with this one	**horiekin**	with them/these
harekin	with that one	**haiekin**	with them/those
hargatik	with that one	**haiengatik**	with them/those

T.N.: Besides being demonstratives, these are also, of course, personal pronouns, although the complete translation has not been given in order to save space. See notes, Lesson 26.

ADITZA

NOR

Inperatiboa

EROR nadin	I must fall
EROR hadi	Fall!
EROR bedi	he must fall
EROR gaitezen	we must fall
EROR zaitez	Fall!
EROR zaitezte	Fall!
EROR bitez	they must fall

GRAMATIK ERREGELAK

"His/her/its" in Basque is "bere" (singular) and "beren" (plural) when it immediately follows the noun to which it refers. If it is separated from its antecedent, the possessive adjective is "haren" (singular) and "haien" (plural). Thus:

gizonak bere txapela eskuan du = the man has his beret in (his) hand.

Relative clauses (often introduced in English by the words "who/which/that") are indicated by adding "-(E)N" to the verb. If the verb to which it is added already ends in "N", an accent mark ("'") is placed over the vowel preceding the "N". Thus:

gizona etorri da = the man has come
etorri den gizona = the man who has come
gizona etorri zen = the man came
etorri zèn gizona = the man who came
ikusi dudan andrea = the woman (whom) I saw

ARIKETAK

Ekarri dudan artoa beserritar hauentzat da	The corn I've brought is for these farmers.
Joan gaitezen etxera lo egitera	Let's go home to sleep.
Etor zaitezte hauekin hitz egitera	Come and speak to them.
Sartu den azkena geldi bedi zutik	The last one to come in must remain standing.
Jar zaitezte eserlekuetan	Take your seats (Seat yourselves on...).
Ken zaitez nire aurretik	Get out of my sight (away from in front of me).
Egon gaitezen hemen geldi	Let's (we must) be quiet here.
Ekarri dituzten erleak arrisku bat dira	The bees they've brought are a danger.
Asma iezaiozu ipuin bat	Make up a story for him.
Irakur iezadazue idazki hori	Read me that text (piece of writing).
Egon zaitez geldi	Be still/quiet.
Zergatik jo zenuen hain gogor?	Why did you hit him so hard?
Gorrotatuko du. Ez du maitatuko	He will hate her. He won't love her.
Etor zaitezte etxera	Come to my house.
Ez zaitezte etorri bihar arte	Don't come until tomorrow.
Izan gaitezen zuzenak	We must be correct (behavior).
Ez gaitezen izan harroak	We mustn't be proud.

HOGEITAZORTZIGARREN IKASGAIA
LESSON TWENTY-EIGHT
HIZTEGIA

honetaz	about this		hauetaz	about these
horretaz	about that		horietaz	about those
* hartaz	about it/that		haietaz	about them/those
honengan	(in/for) this		hauengan	(in/for) these
horrengan	(in/for) that		horiengan	(in/for) those
** harengan	(in/for) that		haiengan	(in/for) those
honengandik	from this		hauengandik	from these
horrengandik	from that		horiengandik	from those
*** harengandik	from that		haiengandik	from those

   * See Gramatik Erregelak, Lesson 18.
  ** See Gramatik Erregelak, Lesson 11.
*** See Gramatik Erregelak, Lesson 19.
    T N.: For further clarification on "Hiztegia" Lessons 26-32, see T.N. Lesson 27.

ADITZA

NOR

Potentzialezko orainaldia

EROR naiteke	I can fall (down)
EROR haiteke	you can fall (down)
EROR daiteke	he can fall (down)
EROR gaitezke	we can fall (down)
EROR zaitezke	you can fall (down)
EROR zaitezkete	you can fall (down)
EROR daitezke	they can fall (down)

Potentzialezko lehenaldia

EROR ninteke	I could/might fall (down)
EROR hinteke	you could/might fall (down)
EROR liteke	he could/might fall (down)
EROR gintezke	we could/might fall (down)
EROR zintezke	you could/might fall (down)
EROR zintezkete	you could/might fall (down)
EROR litezke	they could/might fall (down)

OHARRA.—By adding "-EN" to the past form of the modal verb, we obtain the conditional perfect tense: "I could have fallen down". Thus: nintekeen, etc. Exception: zitekeen (he) and zitezkeen (they), which substitute "l" for "z" at the beginning of the verb. Thus:

> *Eror nintekeen = I could have fallen*
> *Hurbil zintezkeen = you could have come nearer.*

GRAMATIK ERREGELAK

By adding "-TZEN" or "-TEN" to the root (non-finite or tenseless) form of the verb (T.N.: see Gramatik Erregelak, Lesson 26) the progressive or "-ing" form of the verb is obtained. Verbs whose root or non-finite forms end in a vowel or the letters "L" or "R" add "-TZEN". All the others add "-TEN". Thus:

haurra libura apurtzen ari da = the child is breaking the book

Anaia etortzen ari da = my brother is coming

Exception: When the verb ends in **TSI-TZI**, the order is changed from **TS = ST, TZ = ZT**. Thus:

neska janzten ari da = the girl is getting dressed

irakaslea erakusten ari zen = the teacher was teaching.

ARIKETAK

Kontuz!. Eror zaitezke hortik goitik	Be careful! You can fall from up there.
Sar daitezke barrura	They can come in(side).
Liburu hori zikin liteke hor, olio ondoan	That book can get dirty there, next to the oil.
Hartaz hitz egiten ari ginen	We were speaking about that.
Egon zaitezkete hor egun osoan	You can stay there all day.
Erre zaitezke suaz	You can get burned with fire.
Haur hori eror daiteke leihotik behera	That child can/might fall down from the window. (...fall out of...).
Haiengan pentsatzen ari nintzen	I was thinking about them.
Etor zaitezke bihar	You can come tomorrow.
Atzo joan zitekeen	He could have gone yesterday.
Sinesten dut gazte hauengan	I believe in these young people.
Sar zaitezkete ate hartatik	You can enter through that door.
Ez zaitezkete sar ate honetatik	You can't enter throught that door.
Sar al gaitezke ate horretatik?	Can we enter through that door?
Hainbat gauza gerta daiteke	Many things can happen.
Zer gerta daiteke?	What can happen?

HOGEITABEDERATZIGARREN IKASGAIA
LESSON TWENTY-NINE
HIZTEGIA

honengana	to this	hauengana	to these
horrengana	to that	horiengana	to those
harengana	to that/him	haiengana	to those/them
honenganantz	towards this	hauenganantz	towards these
horrenganantz	towards that	horienganantz	towards those
harenganantz	towards that/him	haienganantz	towards those/them
*honenganako	towards him/this one	hauenganako	towards them/these
horrenganako	towards him/that one	horienganako	towards them/those
harenganako	towards him/that one	haienganako	towards them/those

ADITZA

ZER NORK

Inperatiboa

1. NI	1. (TO/AT) ME	**2. HURA**	2. (TO/AT) HIM/HER/IT
IKUS nazazu	Look at me.	IKUS beza	(he must) look at him
IKUS nazazue	Look at me.	IKUS ezazu	Look at him.
		IKUS ezazue	Look at him.
		IKUS bezate	(they must) look at him.

3. GU	3. (TO/AT) US	**4. HAIK**	4. (TO/AT) THEM
IKUS gaitzazu	Look at us	IKUS bitza	(he must) look at them
		IKUS itzazu	Look at them
IKUS gaitzazue	Look at us	IKUS itzazue	Look at them
		IKUS bitzate	(they must) look at them

* T.N.: Honenganako etc., translated in the paradigm as "towards", indicates a relation of feeling rather than direction of movement (indicated by "-ENGANANTZ"), and therefore usually refers to living beings.

GRAMATIK ERREGELAK

Relative clauses introduced by "when" in English are indicated by adding "-(E)NEAN" to the clausal verb. Thus: **nahi dutenean** = when they wish, **nahi dudanean** = when I wish/want. Observe in this last example that the "t" in "dut" has been changed to "d".

Indirect commands are indicated by adding "-TZEKO" to the verb. Thus: **amak esan du etortzeko** = Mother has said for you to come/that you must come (-TEKO) after "**S, Z, X**": **ez hazteko** = not to begin.

ARIKETAK

Gizon harengana joango naiz	I'll go to (where) that man (is).
Ikus ezazu nola datozen hauengana	Look how they are coming to them.
Haienganako maitasuna erakutsi zuen	He showed love towards (for) them.
Nahi duzunean horrengana joango gara	We'll go to him when you wish.
Kontuz ibili ez jausteko	Walk carefully (be careful) so as not to fall.
Esan dit liburu hori ez uzteko	He has told me not to leave that book.
Ikus itzazue birtuteak horiengan	See the virtues in them.
Lagun ezazu gizon eroria	Help the fallen man.
Ikus bitzate injustiziak	(They must) see the injustices.
Maite bezate justizia	(They must) love justice.
Apurtu genituen haienganako loturak	We broke off relations (ties) with them.

Apur itzazue paper zahar horik	Tear up those old papers.
Ekar ezazu zure azken liburua	Bring your last (latest) book.
Eraman itzazu disko hauk	Take these records.
Egin itzazu ikastolarako fitxak	Do the exercises for school.
Ez ezazue utz erlojua gelditzen	Don't let the clock stop.
Ez ezazue gal trena	Don't miss the train.
Ez nazazu utz bakarrik	Don't leave me (here) alone.
Ez bitza eros mapa horik	He musn't buy those maps.
Har bezate gaurko ogia	They must eat today's bread.

HOGEITAMARGARREN IKASGAIA
LESSON THIRTY
HIZTEGIA

honetan	(in etc.) this (place)		hauetan	in these (places)
horretan	(in etc.) that (place)		horietan	in those (places)
hartan	(in etc.) it/that (place)		haietan	in them/those (places)
honetatik	(from etc.) this (place)		hauetatik	from these (places)
horretatik	(from etc.) that (place)		horietatik	from those (places)
hartatik	(from etc.) it/that (place)		haietatik	from them/those (places)
honetara	(to etc.) this (place)		hauetara	to these (places)
horretara	(to etc.) that (place)		horietara	to those (places)
hartara	(to etc.) it/that (place)		haietara	to them/those (places)
ala	or... just/only			
edo	or... also/too			

ADITZA

ZER NORK

Potentzialezko orainaldia		**Potentzialezko orainaldia**	
Hura it		**Haik** them	
APUR dezaket	I can/might break it	APUR ditzaket	I can/might break them
APUR dezakek-n	you can/might break it	APUR ditzakek-n	you can/might break them
APUR dezake	he can/might break it	APUR ditzake	he can/might break them
APUR dezakegu	we can/might break it	APUR ditzakegu	we can/might break them
APUR dezakezu	you can/might break it	APUR ditzakezu	you can/might break them
APUR dezakezue	you can/might break it	APUR ditzakezue	you can/might break them
APUR dezakete	they can/might break it	APUR ditzakete	they can/might break them

GRAMATIK ERREGELAK

The possessive adjectives are formed as follows:

my = **nire, neure** (more intensive) and ene

your (thy) = **hire**

his/her/its = **bere, haren** (when separated from its antecedent)

our = **gure, geure** (intensive)

your (sing.) = **zure, zeure**

your (pl.) = **zuen, zeuen**

their = **beren, haien**

T.N.: The possessive pronouns (mine etc.) are formed by adding the article "-a" to the possessive adjective.

ARIKETAK

Nireak dira, eta apur ditzaket	They are mine and I can break them.
Ene eritziz hau horrela da	In my opinion, it's like that.
Nire eritziz hau horrela da	In my opinion, it's like that.
Horrek ez du nahi bere ohe gainean ezer ipintzea	He doesn't want anything to be put on (over) his bed.
Haren etxea hori da	That is his house (His house is that one).
Horretan ez duzu arrazoirik	You are not right about (in) that.
Bide honetatik oker zoaz	You're taking the wrong road (along this road you're going wrong).
Ipin dezakezu mahaia era honetara	You can set the table this way.
Apur ditzaket paper hauk	I can/might tear up these papers.
Liburu hauetatik zein nahi duzu?	From among these books, which one do you want?
Ezin dezakezu hori egin	You can't do that.
Mahaia gertu dago: ekar dezakezue bazkaria	The table is ready: you can bring the food.
Nahi baduzu, idatz ditzakezu eskutitz horik	If you wish, you can write those letters.
Langile horiek egin dezakete bidea	Those workmen can/might make the road.
Bota ditzakete zuhaitz haik	They might knock those trees down.
Zein etxetàn bizi zara?	In which house do you live?
Etxe hartan bizi gara	We live in that house.
Hau edo (= eta) hori berdin zaizkit	This one or that one, it's the same to me.
Nola etorri zara, trenez ala autoz?	How have you come, by train or by car?
Nola nahi duzu arraultzea, egosita ala frijituta?	How do you want your egg, boiled or fried?
Bata edo (= eta) bestea berdin zaizkit	The one or the other, it's the same to me.
Bata zein bestea, berdin zait	Either one, I don't care.

HOGEITAHAMAIKAGARREN IKASGAIA
LESSON THIRTY-ONE
HIZTEGIA

honetaraino	(up to) this	hauetaraino	(up to) these
horretaraino	(up to) that	horietaraino	(up to) those
* hartaraino	(up to) that/it	haietaraino	(up to) those/them
honetarantz	(towards) this	hauetarantz	(towards) these
horretarantz	(towards) that	horietarantz	(towards) those
hartarantz	(towards) that/it	haietarantz	(towards) those/them
honetarako	(for) this	hauetarako	(for) these
horretarako	(for) that	horietarako	(for) those
** hartarako	(for) that/it	haietarako	(for) those/them
honetako	(of) this	hauetako	(of) these
horretako	(of) that	horietako	(of) those
*** hartako	(of) that/it	haietako	(of) those/them
begiko	nice/kind	honelakorik	something like this
behar	need/must/intend to	horrelakorik	something like that

* See Lesson 19. ** See Lesson 12. *** See Lesson 10.

ADITZA

ZER NORK

Potentzialeko lehenaldia   **Potentzialeko lehenaldia**

Hura	it	Haik	them
APUR nezake	I could/might break it	APUR nitzake	I could/might break them
APUR hezake	you could/might break it	APUR hitzake	you could/might break them
APUR lezake	he could/might break it	APUR litzake	he could/might break them
APUR genezake	we could/might break it	APUR genitzake	we could/might break them
APUR zenezake	you could/might break it	APUR zenitzake	you could/might break them

APUR zenezakete	you could/might break it	APUR zenitzakete	you could/might break them
APUR lezakete	they could/might break it	APUR litzakete	they could/might break them

GRAMATIK ERREGELAK

Frequently in spoken language, the indicative form of the verb plus "ahal" = possibility are used instead of the potential or conditional forms we have just studied. Thus:

hau egin ahal dut ≈ hau egin dezaket = I can do this

hori egin ahal nuen ≈ hori egin nezakeen = I could have done that

ARIKETAK

Apur nezake paper hori baina ez dut horrelakorik egingo	I could tear up that paper but I won't do anything like that.
Hel gaitezke hiri horretaraino	We can get as far as that city.
Joan zaitezkete etxe horretarantz	You can go towards that house.
Ez dizut deitu horretarako	I haven't called you for that (reason).
Herri honetako jendea oso begikoa da	The people in this town are very nice.
Ekar zenitzake jostailu haik	You could/might bring those toys.
Kutxak altxa litzake gora	He could lift the boxes up.
Egin zenezakeen gauzarik hoberena ixilik egotea da	The best thing you could do is to be still.
Eta zuek egin zenezaketena, haizea hartzea	And what you could do is take (a breath of) air.
Zer egin genezake?	What could we do?
Geldirik egon zintezkete	You could be quiet.
Ez naiz etorri honetarako	I haven't come for that. (That's not why I came).
Horrelakorik ez dut inoiz entzun	I've never heard anything like it.
Nahi baduzu, egin dezaket zure ohea	If you wish, I can make your bed.
Ez, oraindik ezin dezakezu egin	No, you can't make it yet (for now).
Beranduago. Geroago. Gero	Later. Afterwards. Later on.
Ikastolan gauza asko ikas genitzake	We could learn many things at school.
Nik eraman nizkien liburu guztiak irakur litzakete	They could read all the books that I took them.
Apur nitzakeen liburuak gero konpondu beharko nituzke	Later I'd have to fix the books I might break.

HOGEITAHAMABIGARREN IKASGAIA
LESSON THIRTY-TWO

HIZTEGIA

hemendik	(from, etc.) here	damu	sorrow
hortik	(from, etc.) there	damutu	be sorry
handik	(from, etc.) (over) there	dardara	vibration
hona	(to) here	dardarti	shaky
horra	(to) there	dardaraz	shake
hara	(to) (over) there	dastatu	try/taste (verbs)
hementxe	right here	debeku	prohibition
hortxe	right there	debekatu	forbid
hantxe	right over there	dei	call (noun)
hemendik zehar	(through) here	deitu	call (verb)
hortik zehar	(through) there	deitura	last name
hor zehar	(through) there	izena	first name
han zehar	(through) there		

ADITZA

NOR

Indikatibozko	baldintza (aurrekoa)	Indikatibozko	baldintza (ondorioa)
banintz	If I were	nintzateke	I would be
bahintz	if you were	hintzateke	you would be
balitz	if he were	litzateke	he would be
bagina	if we were	ginateke	we would be
bazina	if you were	zinateke	you would be
bazinete	if you were	zinatekete	you would be
balira	if they were	lirateke	they would be

GRAMATIK ERREGELAK

"Eta", besides meaning "and", can also be translated as "since/as (because)" when it goes at the end of a clause: **zeren erori baita** ≠ **erori da eta** = since he's fallen.

ARIKETAK

Etorriko bazina, eroriko zinateke	If you came you would fall.
Arin joango balitz, eseriko litzateke	If he went early, he would sit down.
Goiz jaikiko bazinete ikastolara helduko zinatekete	If you got up early you would arrive at school.
Geldi egongo banintz, nire aurrean jarriko zinatekete	If I kept still, you would get in front of me.
Ikastolara joango balira, pozik egongo ginateke	If they went to school we'd be happy.
Horra barrura sartuko banintz, dardarka jarriko nintzateke	If I went in there, I'd start trembling.
Hara gora igongo bazina, damutuko zinateke	If you climbed up there, you'd be sorry.
Debekatuta dagoelako ezin dezakezu hori dasta	You can't try that because it's forbidden.
Zeintzu dira zure izen-deiturak?	What are your first and last names?
Damutu egin zaio etortzea	He's sorry he came.
Debekatu egin zaigu han sartzea	We've been forbidden to go in there.
Joatea. Igotea. Apurtzea	* To go. To climb. To break.
Etor zaitez. Hementxe nago	Come. I'm right here.
Hortxe. Hantxe	Right there. Right over there.
Ginatekenik. Zinatekenik	That we would. That you would.

* T.N.: While these forms most often translate as infinitives, they must be understood as nominalizations of the verb. That is, they function as though they were nouns. For instance, Mendietara joatea ona da = To go to the mountains is good.

33. IKASGAIA – LESSON 33

HIZTEGIA

honela, hola	this way (like this)	egarri	thirst
horrela, hola	that way (like that)	egarri izan	be thirsty
hala	that way (like that)	hegazti	fowl
honetara	this way	egia	the truth
horretara	that way	gezur	false/lie
hartara	that way	iparralde	north
iraun	remain/last	hegoalde	south
baldintza	condition	ekialde	east
desegin	undo/ruin	mendebalde	west
deus	something	egur	fire wood
deus ez	nothing	ehiza	hunting
distira	shine (noun)	ehiztari	hunter
dohain	gift/talent	epe	period of time
dotore	elegant	erabaki	decide
baldar	careless/casual	eragin	promote
hego	wing	eraiki	construct/build
txukundu	fix (up)/improve		

ADITZA

NOR

Subjuntibozko orainaldia

nadin	(so that) I will
hadin	(so that) you will
dadin	(so that) he will
gaitezen	(so that) we will
zaitezen	(so that) you will
zaitezten	(so that) you will
daitezen	(so that) they will

Subjuntibozko lehenaldia

nendin	(so that) I would
hendin	(so that) you would
zedin/ledin	(so that) he would
gintezen	(so that) we would
zintezen	(so that) you would
zintezten	(so that) you would
zitezen/litezen	(so that) they would

OHARRA.—"Nadila, dadila,..." and "nendila, zendila,..." are also employed. In order to distinguish the two forms, remember that "nadin, nendin,..." are used when the clause in English would be introduced by a phrase of the type "so that I will", while "nadila, nendila,..." are used in constructions such as "...that I should/ (for) me to..." (See examples on the following page).

ARIKETAK

Etxea txukundu dute etor zaitezen — They've fixed up the house so that you will come.

Amak esan du etor zaitezela — Mother has said that you should come/for you to come.

Gezurra esan zuten joan nendin — They told a lie so that I would go.

Joan nendila nahi zuten — They wanted me to go.

Ohetik jaikitzerakoan — On getting up (out of bed).

Ea, haurrak, ohetik jaikitzeko ordua da — Hey, kids, it's time to get up.

Zein ordu jo du ordulariak? — What time has the clock struck?

Ikastolarako ordua. Ala, gora! — The hour for (going to) school. Come on, (get) up!

Aurpegia garbitu behar duzue — You must wash your faces.

Ama, gu bakarrik jantziko gara — Mom, we'll get dressed by ourselves.

Bai, zuek bakarrik jantzi behar zarete — Yes, you must get dressed by yourselves.

Irakasleak gu bakarrik jantzi behar garela esan digu — The teacher has told us that we must dress by ourselves.

Bai, horrela izan behar du, handiak zarete eta — Yes, that's the way it's got to be, since you're big (kids now).

Bakoitzak bere ohea egin behar du — Everyone must make his own bed.

Oinetakoak ipin eta lot itzazue — Put your shoes on and tie them.

Ba al dago gosaria? — Is breakfast ready?

Ba al zarete goserik? — Are you hungry?

Bai, gosaria mahai gainean dago — Yes, breakfast is on the table.

Umeak, etor zaitezte gosaria hartzera — Children, come and (to) have breakfast!

Ala, goazen arin kalera, autobusa galdu egingo dugu eta — Come on, let's go outside quick or we'll miss the bus.

Egunotan autobusa berandu etortzen da — The bus is coming late these days.

34 IKASGAIA – LESSON 34

HIZTEGIA

erakutsi	teach/show	**erne**	clever/lively/quick
ezkutatu	hide	**itzarrik**	awake
erantzi	undress	**lotan**	asleep
erantsi	add/stick/join	**loak hartu**	fall asleep
erauzi	extract/take out	**ero**	lunatic
eraztun	ring	**eroturik**	crazy
erbi	hare	**errota**	mill
eredu	model	**errotari**	miller
erein	sow (verb)	**eskatu**	ask for
eremu	desert	**eskakizun**	request
eri	sick person	**eskuin**	right
eritegi	hospital	**ezker**	left
heriotza	death	**estali**	cover (up)

ADITZA

ZER NORI NORK

Potentzialezko orainaldia

Hura   it

EMAN diezaioket	I can give it to him
EMAN diezaioke	he can give it to him
EMAN diezaiokegu	we can give it to him
EMAN diezaiokezu	you can give it to him
EMAN diezaiokezue	you can give it to him
EMAN diezaiokete	they can give it to him

Potentzialezko orainaldia

Hura   it

EMAN diezaieket	I can give it to them
EMAN diezaieke	he can give it to them
EMAN diezaiekegu	we can give it to them
EMAN diezaiekezu	you can give it to them
EMAN diezeiekezue	you can give it to them
EMAN diezeiekete	they can give it to them

OHARRA.—If what is being given is not one thing (it) but several (them), the auxiliary verb must begin with "diezazki" instead of "dieza": EMAN diezazkioket, EMAN diezazkioke,...

ARIKETAK

Ondo portatu behar zara, hemen iraun zaitezen
You must behave well so you can stay here.

Joan zaitezkete ehizara hegoalderantz
To hunt, you can go (towards the) south.

Erabaki bat hartu behar zenukete
You should make up your minds (take a decision).

Ezin diezaiokezu nori esan
You can't say that to him.

Eska diezaieke egia esatea eta ez gezurrak
They can ask them to tell the truth (what's true) and not lie (what's false).

IKASTOLATIK ETORTZERAKOAN
ARRIVING FROM SCHOOL

Aita, irakasleak fitxak egiteko agindu dit
Father, the teacher has told me to do exercises.

Ea, atera itzazu papera eta boligrafoa
Well, get out (some) paper and a pen.

Hemen ditut. Atera ditut.
I've got them here. I've taken them out.

Irakur ezazu fitxa
Read the exercise.

Orain irakurriko dizut
I'll read it to you now.

Orain irakurriko dizkizut
I'll read them to you now.

Ez dut ulertzen. Ez dizut ulertzen
I don't understand it. I don't understand you.

Irakur ezazu berriz ere, baina astiro
Read it again, but slowly.

Bai, orain ulertzen dizut
Yes, now I understand you.

Ba, idatz ezazu erantzuna
Well, write the answer.

Idatz itzazu galderen erantzunak
Write the answers to the questions.

Zuk esan nola idatzi behar ditudan
You tell me how I must write them.

Ez, hori zuk egin behar duzu
No, you are the one who must do that.

Hori zuk egin behar duzun lana da
That is work which you must do.

Baina ez dakit
But I don't know how.

Idatz ezazu dakizun bezala, eta gero nik emango diot begirada bat
Write the way you know how, and then I'll have a look at it (give it a look).

35 IKASGAIA – LESSON 35
HIZTEGIA

hiltzaile	murderer	**ezkondu**	get married
ikertzaile	investigator	**eskuratu**	reach/achieve/obtain
hilketa	murder (noun)	**eztarri**	throat
susmagarri	suspect	**ezkontza**	wedding
eragingarri	motive	**eztul**	cough (noun)
xantaia	blackmail	**fede**	faith
etsai	enemy	**finkatu**	establish
euli	fly (insect)	**froga**	proof
ezagun	acquaintance	**funts**	basis
ezarri	put/set/place	**gabe**	without

ADITZA
ZER NORI NORK

Potentzialezko orainaldia

Potentzialezko orainaldia

Hura	it	**Hura**	it
EMAN diezadake	he can give it to me	**EMAN diezaguke**	he can give it to us
EMAN diezadakezu	you can give it to me	**EMAN diezagukezu**	you can give it to us
EMAN diezadakezue	you can give it to me	**EMAN diezagukezue**	you can give it to us
EMAN diezadakete	they can give it to me	**EMAN diezagukete**	they can give it to us

Hura	it	**Hura**	it
EMAN diezazuket	I can give it to you	**EMAN diezazueket**	I can give it to you
EMAN diezazuke	he can give it to you	**EMAN diezazueke**	he can give it to you
EMAN diezazukegu	we can give it to you	**EMAN diezazuekegu**	we can give it to you
EMAN diezazukete	they can give it to you	**EMAN diezazuekete**	they can give it to you

OHARRA.—If the direct object (it) is plural (them), the auxiliary verb begins with "diezazki" instead of "dieza": EMAN diezazkidake, EMAN diezazkidakezu,...

ARIKETAK

Nahi duzunean dei egin diezadakezu	You can call me when you wish.
Ez diezagukezu ikus bihar arte	You can't see us until tomorrow.
Eskatutako dokumentuak ekar diezazki-gukete	They can bring us the requested documents.
Paristik ekarritako eraztunak erakuts die-zazkigukezue	You can show us the rings brought from Paris.
Ehiztariak hildako erbiak ipin diezazki-zuekete	They can serve you the hares the hunter shot.

TELEBISTA IKUSTERAKOAN

WATCHING TELEVISION

Ama, telebista ikusi nahi dut	Mom, I want to watch television.
Baina lehenago jatekoa amaitu behar duzu	But first you must finish eating.
Amaitu dut. Bukatu dut	I've finished.
Ez, laranja hori jan behar duzu	No, you must eat that orange.
Ez dut laranja jateko gogorik	I don't feel like eating the orange.
Ondo, ipin ezazu telebista	Very well, turn the TV on.
Telebista gehiegi ikustea ez da ona. Kalte-garria da	Watching TV too much isn't good. It's bad for you.
Eta zergatik da kaltegarria?	And why is it bad for you?
Begietarako ez da ona, eta, gainera, pertso-na moteldu egiten da, alferra bihurtzen da	It's not good for the eyes, and besides, the viewer is made less lively* and becomes lazy.
Gehiegikeriak ez dira onak izaten	Excesses are not good.
Baina ez dugu gehiegi ikusiko. Filme bat soilik	But we won't watch too much. Only one film.
Ipin ezazu telebista. Ken ezazu	Turn the TV on. Turn it off.
Ipin ezazu ozenkiago. Ipin beherago	Turn it up (louder). Turn it down.
Irudiak ez dira ongi ikusten	The picture isn't clear. (The images...).
Ez da argi entzuten	The sound doesn't come through clearly.
Ipin ezazu bigarren katea	Turn it to the second channel.

---

* T.N.: Note that the closest approximation to the passive voice in Basque occurs when a transitive verb is conjugated with the auxiliary IZAN rather than UKAN. Thus, Hemen liburu asko saltzen dute = They sell many books here, whereas Liburu asko saltzen da = Many books are sold.

36 IKASGAIA – LESSON 36

HIZTEGIA

garraio	transportation	gaztelu	castle
garraiatu	transport	gazteria	youth
garratz	bitter/sour	gerezi	cherry
gartzela	jail	gerizpe	shade/shadow
atxilotu	arrest	gerri	waist
gatz	salt	gerriko	belt
azukre	sugar	gertu	ready/prepared
gazi	salty	gozo	sweet/rich
gazta	cheese	gibel	liver
gaztaina	chestnut	goibel	grey/sad/overcast
goilare	spoon		

ADITZA

ZER NORI NORK

Potentzialezko lehenaldia

Hura   it

EMAN niezaioke	I could give it to him
EMAN liezaioke	he could give it to him
EMAN geniezaioke	we could give it to him
EMAN zeniezaioke	you could give it to him

EMAN zeniezaiokete	you could give it to him
EMAN liezaiokete	they could give it to him

Potentzialezko lehenaldia

Hura   it

EMAN niezaieke	I could give it to them
EMAN liezaieke	he could give it to them
EMAN geniezaieke	we could give it to them
EMAN zeniezaieke	you could give it to them

EMAN zeniezaiekete	you could give it to them
EMAN liezaiekete	they could give it to them

OHARRA.—These forms are for singular direct object (it). When the direct object is plural, the verb is: niezazkioke, liezazkioke,...

ARIKETAK

Zuhaitz honek eman liezaiokeen gerizpea ez litzateke handia izango
The shade this tree could give him wouldn't be very big.

Nahi luketen gazta guztia eman geniezaieke
We could give them all the cheese they wanted.

Fedea ekintzetan frogatu behar luke
He must show (his) faith with deeds.

Zertan finka dezakezu zeure eritzia?
What can you base your opinion on?

Horrek ez du funtsik
That has no meaning (foundation).

Funtsik gabeko arrazoia da hori
That is a reason without foundation.

Gatza gazia da eta azukrea gozoa
Salt is salty and sugar, sweet.

Haiek gartzelara eraman litzakete
They could take them to jail.

IGANDEA ETORTZERAKOAN
WHEN SUNDAY COMES

Bihar igandea da. Nora joan gaitezke?
Tomorrow is Sunday. Where can we go?

Bihar jaieguna denez, mendira joan gaitezke
Since tomorrow is a day off, we can go to the country (to the mountains).

Ez, hobe automobilean joango bagina
No, (it would be) better if we went by car.

Baina, nora joan gintezke?
But, where could we go?

Elurretara. Ez, itsas portu bat ikustera
To the snow. No, to see a fishing village (port).

Mendi portuak hertsirik daudelako ezin gaitezke elurretara joan
We can't go to the snow because the mountain passes are closed.

Kotxeak pasatzeko kateak ipini behar zaizkie, eta guk ez dugu katerik
Cars, in order to pass (get through), must have chains put on, and we don't have any chains.

Eta itsas portuan hotz egingo du
And it will be cold in the fishing village.

Orduan, etxean geratuko al gara?
Then, shall we stay at home?

Ez, pilotaleku batetara joango bagina, pilotan egingo genuke
No, if we went to a ball court we would play ball.

Hona edo hara, nonbaitera joan beharko dugu. Beraz, jantz zaitezte
One place or another, we'll have to go somewhere. So, get dressed.

37 IKASGAIA — LESSON 37

HIZTEGIA

gona	skirt	**higuin**	nauseating
gor	deafness/deaf person	**ihintz**	dew
goraintziak	greetings, regards	**ikaratu**	be frightened
gordin	raw	**lurrikara**	earthquake
gorringo	yolk	**hildo**	row/line
zuringo	egg white	**hildo beretik**	along this line
grina	passion	**inhurri**	ant
gupida	compassion	**ireki**	open
gurtu	venerate	**irentsi**	swallow
gurutze	cross (noun)	**intzaur**	walnut
ihes egin	escape/run away	**urrak**	hazel nuts
iragan	pass	**irin**	flour
igeri egin	swim	**ito**	drown/smother

ADITZA

ZER NORI NORK

Potentzialezko lehenaldia

Hura *it*

EMAN liezadake he could give it to me
EMAN zeniezadake you could give it to me

EMAN zeniezadakete you could give it to me
EMAN liezadakete they could give it to me

Hura *it*

EMAN niezazuke I could give it to you

EMAN liezazuke he could give it to you

EMAN geniezazuke we could give it to you

EMAN liezazukete they could give it to you

Potentzialezko lehenaldia

Hura *it*

EMAN liezaguke he could give it to us
EMAN zeniezaguke you could give it to us

EMAN zeniezagukete you could give it to us
EMAN liezagukete they could give it to us

Hura *it*

EMAN niezazueke I could give it to you

EMAN liezazueke he could give it to you

EMAN geniezazueke we could give it to you

EMAN liezazuekete they could give it to you

OHARRA.—As always, these forms are for singular direct objects. When the direct object is plural, the verb is: liezazkidake, zeniezazkidake,...

ARIKETAK

Gorantziak eman liezazkiguke — They could/might give (send) us regards.

Atea ireki behar zeniezadake — You might open the door for me.

Ekar zeniezazkiguketen intzaurrak ez lirateke onak izango — The walnuts you might bring wouldn't be good.

Gorringoa eman zeniezadake eta gorde dezakezu zuringoa — You could give me the yolk and you can keep the white of the egg.

Gupida gabe jo zuen — He hit him without compassion.

OHERA JOATERAKOAN — GOING TO BED

Berandu da, eta jantz itzazue pijamak — It's late, and put your pyjamas on.

Baina oraindik ez dira bederatzirak. Goizegi da — But it's not nine yet. It's too early.

Ez da goizegi. Umeek lo asko egin behar dute — It's not too early. Children must sleep a lot.

Ken ezazue telebista, eta goazen ohera — Turn the TV off and let's go to bed.

Formal bazatoze ipuin polit bat kondatuko dizuet — If you come nicely (without a fuss), I'll tell you a good story.

Ez, nahiago dugu igarkizun batzu esatea — No, we'd rather tell some riddles.

Zerbait kantatzea nahiago dut — I'd rather sing something.

Ondo, dena den, goazen ohera eta bertan kontseilu bat egingo dugu — Well, anyway, let's go to bed and we'll have a discussion.

Kontseiluan erabakiko dugu zer egingo dugun — During the discussion we'll decide what we're going to do.

Lehen otoitz labur bat — First a short prayer.

Igarkizun bat esango dizuet, eta ezetz igarri zer den — I'm going to tell you a riddle and I bet you won't guess what it is.

Ni logura naiz — I'm sleepy.

Ba, ni ez naiz oraindik logurarik — Well I'm not sleepy yet.

Orain lo egin behar duzue. Musu bana emango dizuet — Now you must go to sleep. I'll give you each a kiss.

38 IKASGAIA – LESSON 38
HIZTEGIA

itsu	blind person	**luze**	long
gor	deaf person	**larri**	troublesome
iturri	fountain	**lasto**	straw
itxura	appearance	**lotsa**	shame
izter	thigh	**askatu**	let loose/release
jaio	be born	**lotu**	tie (verb)
jarraitu, jarraiki	continue	**luma**	feather
josi	sew	**moko**	beak
kutsu	flavor	**buztan**	tail
euskal kutsu	Basque flavor	**marinel**	sailor
labe	oven	**molde**	manner
eskean	begging	**ondorio**	consequence/result
eskatu	ask for		

ADITZA
ZER NORK

Indikatibozko baldintza (aurrekoa)   **Indikatibozko baldintza (aurrekoa)**

Hura	it	**Haik**	them
IKUSIKO banu	if I saw it	**IKUSIKO banitu**	if I saw them
IKUSIKO bahu	if you saw it	**IKUSIKO bahitu**	if you saw them
IKUSIKO balu	if he saw it	**IKUSIKO balitu**	if he saw them
IKUSIKO bagenu	if we saw it	**IKUSIKO bagenitu**	if we saw them
IKUSIKO bazenu	if you saw it	**IKUSIKO bazenitu**	if you saw them
IKUSIKO bazenute	if you saw it	**IKUSIKO bazenituzte**	if you saw them
IKUSIKO balute	if they saw it	**IKUSIKO balituzte**	if they saw them

Indikatibozko baldintza (ondorioa)   **Indikatibozko baldintza (ondorioa)**

Hura	it	**Haik**	them
IKUSIKO nuke	I would see it	**IKUSIKO nituzke**	I would see them
IKUSIKO huke	you would see it	**IKUSIKO hituzke**	you would see them
IKUSIKO luke	he would see it	**IKUSIKO lituzke**	he would see them
IKUSIKO genuke	we would see it	**IKUSIKO genituzke**	we would see them
IKUSIKO zenuke	you would see it	**IKUSIKO zenituzke**	you would see them
IKUSIKO zenukete	you would see it	**IKUSIKO zenituzkete**	you would see them
IKUSIKO lukete	they would see it	**IKUSIKO lituzkete**	they would see them

ARIKETAK

Itsu bat eskean ikusiko banu, dirua emango nioke
If I saw a blind man begging, I'd give him money.

Txoriek kolore askotako lumak dituzte
Birds have many-colored feathers.

Marinel horren izterrak ikusiko bazenitu lodiak direla aitortuko zenidake
If you saw that sailor's thighs, you'd admit they're fat.

Asko irakurriko balute, ondorio onak aterako lituzkete
If they read a lot, they'd get good results.

DENDARIK DENDA

GOING SHOPPING

Eguraldi ona dagoenez gero, dendarik denda joan gaitezke
Since the weather is good we can go shopping.

Zer erosi behar duzu, ba?
What are you going to buy, then? (What do you have to buy?).

Hainbat gauza erosi behar nuke, baina ez dut denetarako diru nahikorik
I was going to buy many things, but I don't have enough money for all of them.

Zenbat balio du jantzi honek?
How much does this dress cost?

Jantzi honek bi mila pezeta balio ditu
This dress costs two thousand pesetas.

Garestiegia da. Merkeagotu diezadakezu?
It's too expensive. Can you give me a better price? (make it cheaper for me?).

Har ezazu kontuan, asko merkeagotu dugula
As a matter of fact, we've already brought the price way down (lowered it a lot).

Orain bi hilabete, hiru mila balio zuen
Two months ago it cost three thousand.

Dena den, orain ere garestia iruditzen zait
Anyhow, it still seems expensive to me.

Garestia dela uste duzu?
Do you think it's expensive?

Horrela da
That's right (that's the way it is).

Ondo ba. Ehuneko hamarra kenduko dizut
O.K., then. I'll take off ten percent.

Prezio honetan hartuko dizut
I'll take it at that price.

39 IKASGAIA — LESSON 39

HIZTEGIA

muga	limit/border/frontier	**oporrak**	vacation
higitu	move (verb)	**oroitu**	remember
mugitu	feel/be moved	**orratz**	needle
higidura	movement (physical)	**josi**	sew
mugimendu	movement (physical and spiritual)	**oihal**	material/cloth
multzo	set (noun)	**orrazi**	comb (noun)
mutu	mute	**orraztu**	comb (verb)
mutur	end/extreme		
zapata	shoe		
nahasi	mixture/mix (noun and verb)	**hospe**	fame/reputation
nabari	notorious	**ostatu**	village inn
oker	wrong/crooked		
zuzen	right/straight		

ADITZA

ZER NORK

Indikatibozko baldintza (aurrekoa) **Indikatibozko baldintza (aurrekoa)**

Ni

Gu

IKUSIKO banindu	if he saw me	**IKUSIKO bagintu**	if he saw us
IKUSIKO baninduzu	if you saw me	**IKUSIKO bagintuzu**	if you saw us
IKUSIKO baninduzue	if you saw me	**IKUSIKO bagintuzue**	if you saw us
IKUSIKO banindute	if they saw me	**IKUSIKO bagintuzte**	if they saw us

Indikatibozko baldintza (ondorioa) **Indikatibozko baldintza (ondorioa)**

Ni

Gu

IKUSIKO ninduke	he would see me	**IKUSIKO gintuzke**	he would see us
IKUSIKO nindukezu	you would see me	**IKUSIKO gintuzkezu**	you would see us
IKUSIKO nindukezue	you would see me	**IKUSIKO gintuzkezue**	you would see us
IKUSIKO nindukete	they would see me	**IKUSIKO gintuzkete**	they would see us

ARIKETAK

Bart ikusi baninduzu harrituko zinatekeen — If you had seen me last night, you would have been frightened.

Erori zèn euriaz guztiz busti nintzen — I got completely soaked by the rain that fell.

Zuen automobilean eramango bagintuzue, arinago helduko ginateke — If you took us in your car we would get there quicker.

Oihalak, orratz honetaz josi beharko zenituzke — You should sew the material with this needle.

Hospe handiko ostatu batetara joango bazina, mututurik geratuko zinateke — If you went to an inn with a big reputation, you'd be left speechless.

BIZARTEGIAN — AT THE BARBER SHOP

Ilea moztu nahi dut — I want to cut my hair (have it cut).

Asko ala guti? — A lot or a little?

Orain ile luzea modan dago — Long hair is in style now.

Horrek zera esan nahi du, guti ebaki behar dudala, ez da? — That means I must cut very little, doesn't it?

Eta, bizarra? — And your beard?

Ez, bizarra utz ezazu dagoen bezala — No, leave my beard as it is.

Bustiko al dizut burua? — Shall I wet your head?

Ez, hotz dago eta — No, because it's cold.

Zenbat zor dizut? — How much do I owe you?

Berrogeitahamar pezeta — Fifty pesetas.

Ez dut ganbiorik, eta ehuneko bat emango dizut — I don't have any change, and I'll give you a one-hundred (peseta bill).

Beste berrogeitahamar pezeta bihurtu behar dizkidazu — You must give me the other 50 pesetas back.

Nor jarraitzen da orain? — Who is next?

40 IKASGAIA — LESSON 40

HIZTEGIA

ostiko	kick (noun)	**porru**	leek
hots	noise	**premia**	need
piku	fig	**prest, gertu**	ready/prepared
pitxer	pitcher	**sagu**	mouse
pisu	weight	**saiatu**	try (verb)
pisatu	weigh	**salatu**	denounce/report
pix	urine	**samur**	tender
plater	plate	**sare**	net
edalontzi	glass	**sarri, maiz**	often

ADITZA

ZER NORK

Indikatibozko baldintza (aurrekoa)   **Indikatibozko baldintza (aurrekoa)**

Zu   **Zuek**

IKUSIKO bazintut	if I saw you	**IKUSIKO bazintuztet**	if I saw you
IKUSIKO bazintu	if he saw you	**IKUSIKO bazintuzte**	if he saw you
IKUSIKO bazintugu	if we saw you	**IKUSIKO bazintuztegu**	if we saw you
IKUSIKO bazintuzte	if they saw you	**IKUSIKO bazintuztete**	if they saw you

Indikatibozko baldintza (ondorioa)   **Indikatibozko baldintza (ondorioa)**

Zu   **Zuek**

IKUSIKO zintuzket	I would see you	**IKUSIKO zintuzketet**	I would see you
IKUSIKO zintuzke	he would see you	**IKUSIKO zintuzkete**	he would see you
IKUSIKO zintuzkegu	we would see you	**IKUSIKO zintuzketegu**	we would see you
IKUSIKO zintuzkete	they would see you	**IKUSIKO zintuzketete**	they would see you

ARIKETAK

Okerkeriak egiten ikusi bazintut ostiko bat emango nizuke
If I saw you doing bad things, I'd give you a kick.

Piku horiek gutiago pisatuko balute gehiago erosiko nituzke
If these figs weighed less, I'd buy more.

Katua sagua harrapatzen saiatu da, baina alferrik
The cat is trying to catch the mouse, but in vain.

Zurekin egoteko premia dut. Zerbait salatu behar nizun
I need to be with you. I had something to report to you.

Horrela ikusiko bazintuztete, harrituko lirateke
If they saw you like that, they'd be amazed.

Etorriko bazinete ikusiko zenituzkete
If you came you would see them.

AUTOBUSEAN

ON THE BUS

Nora doa autobus hau?
Where is this bus going?

Eta zeintzu kaletatik doa?
And along which streets does it go?

Ni azkeneraino noa, eta zu?
I'm going to the end of the line, and you?

Nik ez dakit ongi non jaitsi behar naizen
I don't know for sure where I must get off.

Lehenengoz hartzen dut autobus hau
I'm taking this bus for the first time.

Azkeneraino noanez, nik non jaitsi behar zaren esango dizut
Since I'm going to the end of the line, I'll tell you where you must get off.

Eskerrik asko. Ez dago zergatik
Thanks very much. Not at all. Don't mention it.

Non jaitsi behar zara?
Where are you getting off?

Merkatuaren inguruan
Near the market.

Ba ote dago eserlekurik?
Are there any seats?

Bai, hirurentzat dago
Yes, there is room for three.

Ez, laurentzat
No, for four.

Sar al gaitezke?
Can we get on?

Ez, ezin zaitezkete sar. Dena beterik dago
No, you can't get on. It's all full.

Hemen jaitsi nahi dut. Gera, mesedez
I want to get off here. Please stop.

PART TWO

In Part Two there are complete charts of verbs and declensions. The most commonly used verbal forms have already been presented in the forty previous lessons.

The Basque auxiliary verb distinguishes in its different forms the subject of a transitive verb (NORK), the indirect object or "dative of interest" of transitive and intransitive verbs (NORI), and the direct objects (inanimate or personal) which in Basque fall under the headings ZER, NOR. The four verbal types are therefore represented as:

1. NOR (who). Ex.: ni naiz (I am).
2. NOR NORI (who-to/for whom). Ex.: ni zuri hurbiltzen natzaizu (I come to you).
3. ZER NORK (what-who). Ex.: nik zu ikusi zaitut (I have seen you).
4. ZER NORI NORK (what-to/for whom-who). Ex.: nik zuri liburua ekarri dizut (I've brought you the book).

In Part Two you will find charts for groups 2, 3, and 4. Group No. 1 has been included in its entirety in Part One of this book.

NOR - NORI

*NOR - NORI

2.1.- Indikatibozko orainaldia

Hurbildu natzaio. = I have come to him.
Hurbilduko natzaio = I will come to him.
Hurbiltzen natzaio = I come to him.

	NIRI	HIRI	HARI	GURI	ZURI	ZUEI	HAIEI
NI		natzaik / natzain	natzaio		natzaizu	natzaizue	natzaie
HI	hatzait		hatzaio	hatzaigu			hatzaie
HURA	**zait**	**zaik / zain**	**zaio**	**zaigu**	**zaizu**	**zaizue**	**zaie**
GU		gatzaizkik / gatzaizkin	gatzaizkio		gatzaizkizu	gatzaizkizue	gatzaizkie
ZU	zatzaizkit		zatzaizkio	zatzaizkigu			zatzaizkie
ZUEK	zatzaizkidate		zatzaizkiote	zatzaizkigute			zatzaizkiete
HAIK	**zaizkit**	**zaizkik / zaizkin**	**zaizkio**	**zaizkigu**	**zaizkizu**	**zaizkizue**	**zaizkie**

OHARRA.—In these charts, the verbs written in heavy print are the most commonly used forms of the conjugation.

ARIKETAK

Hitz egiteko asmoz hurbildu natzaio baina ez dit jaramonik egin	I've come to him with the intention of speaking to him, but he hasn't paid any attention to me.
Erori egin zaizkit platerak	I've dropped the plates. (The plates have fallen re: me).
Erori zaizkidan platerak apurtu egin dira	The plates I've dropped are broken (...have become broken) See T.N., Lesson 35, ARIKETAK.
Gure zereginari lotu gatzaizkio	We've tied ourselves to our work.
Zer gertatu zaio?	What has happened to him?
Ez dakit zer gertatu zaien	I don't know what has happened to them.
Astiro ez badabil, erori egingo zaizkio	If he doesn't walk slowly, he's going to drop them (they'll fall re: him).
Gordetzen ez badituzte, galdu egingo zaizkie	If they don't put them away, they'll get lost (re: them).
Erlojuei kordelik ematen ez badiezue, geldituko zaizkizue	If you don't wind the clocks up, they will stop (re: you).
Noiz gureganatuko zatzaizkigute?	When will we get you to be with us?
Inoiz ez gatzaizkizue zuenganatuko	You'll never get us to be with you.
Horrelakoak izateagatik, hainbat problema sortu zaie	Because they are like that (for being like that), so many problems have arisen for them.
Buruhausteak sortu zaizkie	Many problems (headaches) have come up for them.

* See T.N., Lesson 15.

NOR - NORI

2.2.- Indikatibozko lehenaldia

Hurbildu nintzaion	= I came to him.
Hurbilduko nintzaion	= I would have come to him.
Hurbiltzen nintzaion	= I came (used to come) to him.

	NIRI	HIRI	HARI	GURI	ZURI	ZUEI	HAIEI
NI		nintzaian / nintzainan	nintzaion		nintzaizun	nintzaizuen	nintzaien
HI	hintzaidan		hintzaion	hintzaigun			hintzaien
HURA	zitzaidan	zitzaian / zitzainan	zitzaion	zitzaigun	zitzaizun	zitzaizuen	zitzaien
GU		gintzaizkian / gintzaizkinan	gintzaizkion		gintzaizkizun	gintzaizkizuen	gintzaizkien
ZU	zintzaizkidan		zintzaizkion	zintzaizkigun			zintzaizkien
ZUEK	zintzaizkidaten		zintzaizkioten	zintzaizkiguten			zintzaizkieten
HAIK	zitzaizkidan	zitzaizkian / zitzaizkinan	zitzaizkion	zitzaizkigun	zitzaizkizun	zitzaizkizuen	zitzaizkien

ARIKETAK

Deitu ninduenean (zidanean) berehala hurbildu nintzaion

Arreta handiz lotu gintzaizkion euskara ikasteari

Nahi gabe apurtu zitzaizkien platerak

Atzo paper hauk erori zitzaizkizun

Lehengusuak etorri zitzaizkizuen

Zuk esan bezala, joan nintzaion

Bere besoetara erori zitzaion

Ez dakizu nolako ipuinekin etorri zitzaizkigun!

Etxera etorri zitzaizkigun baina ez geunden

Orduan gu joan gintzaizkizun

Gauza barregarriak gertatu zitzaizkien

Automobila apurtu zitzaion

Noiz etorri zitzaizun anaia?

Bart etorri zitzaidan

Ez zitzaizun atsegin izango haiekin egotea

When he called me, I came to him right away.

With great attention we devote ourselves to the learning of Basque.

They broke the dishes without meaning to.

Yesterday you dropped those papers.

Your cousins came.

Just as you said, I went to him.

It (he, she) fell into his arms.

They came to us with you-don't-know-how-many stories.

They came to us at home, but we weren't there.

Therefore, we went to them.

Funny things happened to them.

His car broke down.

When did your brother come?

He came last night.

You wouldn't have enjoyed being with them. (Being with them wouldn't have been pleasing to you).

NOR - NORI

Hurbildu banintzaio = if I had come to him.

Hurbilduko banintzaio = if I came to him.

2.3.- Indikatibozko baldintza (aurrekoa)

	NIRI	HIRI	HARI	GURI	ZURI	ZUEI	HAIEI
NI		banintzaik / banintzain	banintzaio		banintzaizu	banintzaizue	banintzaie
HI	bahintzait		bahintzaio	bahintzaigu			bahintzaie
HURA	balitzait	balitzaik / balitzain	balitzaio	balitzaigu	balitzaizu	balitzaizue	balitzaie
GU		bagintzaizkik / bagintzaizkin	bagintzaizkio		bagintzaizkizu	bagintzaizkizue	bagintzaizkie
ZU	bazintzaizkit		bazintzaizkio	bazintzaizkigu			bazintzaizkie
ZUEK	bazintzaizkidate		bazintzaizkiote	bazintzaizkigute			bazintzaizkiete
HAIK	balitzaizkit	balitzaizkik / balitzaizkin	balitzaizkio	balitzaizkigu	balitzaizkizu	balitzaizkizue	balitzaizkie

ARIKETAK

Basque	English
Horrelakorik gertatuko balitzait, urduri nengoke	If something like that happened to me, I would be upset.
Kutxa hori buru gainera eroriko balitzaio, hil egingo litzateke	If that box fell on his head, he would be killed.
Edalontziak apurtuko balitzaizkie, ezingo lukete urik edan	If their (drinking) glasses broke, they wouldn't be able to drink any water.
Platerak apurtuko balitzaizkizue, ezina gertatuko litzaizueke bazkaltzea	If your plates got broken, it would be impossible for you to make lunch.
Liburu horik galduko balitzaizkizue , ezina izango litzaizueke beste horrelakorik lortzea	If those books got lost, it would be impossible for you to find any (others) like them.
Koadroak eroriko balitzaizkigu, apurtuko lirateke	If the pictures fell (re: us), they would break.
Zer egingo zenuke anaia etorriko balitzaizu?	What would you do if your brother came?
Anaia etorriko balitzait, guztiz (asko) poztuko nintzateke	If my brother came, I would be happy.
Leiala izango bazintzaizkio, eskertuko lizuke	If you were loyal to him, he would be very grateful to you.

NOR - NORI

2.4.- Indikatibozko baldintza (ondorioa)   Hurbilduko nintzaioke = I would come to him.

	NIRI	HIRI	HARI	GURI	ZURI	ZUEI	HAIEI
NI		nintzaiake / nintzainake	nintzaioke		nintzaizuke	nintzaizueke	nintzaieke
HI	hintzaidake		hintzaioke	hintzaiguke			hintzaieke
HURA	litzaidake	litzaiake / litzainake	litzaioke	litzaiguke	litzaizuke	litzaizueke	litzaieke
GU		gintzaizkiake / gintzaizkinake	gintzaizkioke		gintzaizkizuke	gintzaizkizueke	gintzaizkieke
ZU	zintzaizkidake		zintzaizkioke	zintzaizkiguke			zintzaizkieke
ZUEK	zintzaizkidakete		zintzaizkiokete	zintzaizkigukete			zintzaizkiekete
HAIK	litzaizkidake	litzaizkiake / litzaizkinake	litzaizkioke	litzaizkiguke	litzaizkizuke	litzaizkizueke	litzaizkieke

ARIKETAK

Koadro honi gehigarri batzu zor litzaizkioke

For this picture, some additions would be necessary.

Horien artean neure burua agertzea lotsagarri litzaidake

To appear in their midst (company) would be shameful for me.

Nire lagunari ez litzaioke axola hirira joatea

My friend wouldn't mind going to the city (Going to the city wouldn't matter to my friend).

Oso zaila izango litzaidake honelako adiskide bat bilatzea

To (have to) look for another friend like him would be very difficult for me.

Zer gertatuko litzaiguke lanik egingo ez bagenu?

What would happen to us if we didn't work?

Kezkagarri izan behar litzaizkieke burrukak

The fights must have been worrisome for them.

Kostatuko litzaidake hori sinestea

It would cost me (quite an effort) to believe that.

Kontuz ibiliko ez bagina, eroriko litzaizkiguke

If we weren't careful (...didn't walk carefully) we would drop them.

Nahi bazenute, elkartuko gintzaizkizueke

If you wanted (us to), we would join you.

Harrera onik banu, joango nintzaizuke etxera

If I received a good welcome, I would go to your house.

NOR - NORI

2.5.- Potentzialezko orainaldia   Hurbil nakioke   = I can/may come to him.

	NIRI	HIRI	HARI	GURI	ZURI	ZUEI	HAIEI
NI		nakiake / nakinake	nakioke		nakizuke	nakizueke	nakieke
HI	hakidake		hakioke	hakiguke			hakieke
HURA	dakidake	dakiake dakinake	dakioke	dakiguke	dakizuke	dakizueke	dakieke
GU		gakizkiake / gakizkinake	gakizkioke		gakizkizuke	gakizkizueke	gakizkieke
ZU	zakizkidake		zakizkioke	zakizkiguke			zakizkieke
ZUEK	zakizkidakete		zakizkiokete	zakizkigukete			zakizkiekete
HAIK	dakizkidake	dakizkiake / dakizkinake	dakizkioke	dakizkiguke	dakizkizuke	dakizkizueke	dakizkieke

ARIKETAK

Kontuz, eror dakiguke eta	Be careful, since it may fall (re: us).
Idazten ez badut ahantz dakidake	I may forget it if I don't write it down.
Horra gora igoten badituzu jaus dakiz-kizuke	If you put them up there, they may fall.
Etor zakizkidake etxera bisitatzera	You can come to visit me at home.
Hurbil dakidake nahi duenean	He can come to me when he wants.
Esan iezaiezue hurbil dakizkidakeela nahi dutenean	Tell them that they can come to me when they want.
Esan dit elkar nakizuekeela	He has told me that I may join you.
Eror dakizkiguke gainean, eta gero, zer?	They can fall on us, and then what?
Joan nakieke ikustera	I can go see them.
Etor zakizkidake dirua ordaintzeko	You can come to me to pay the money.
Jaus dakizuke pitxer hori mahai gai-netik	That pitcher (of yours) might fall off the table. (= it might be your fault).

NOR - NORI

2.6.- Potentzialezko lehenaldia   Hurbil nenkioke   = I could/might come to him.

	NIRI	HIRI	HARI	GURI	ZURI	ZUEI	HAIEI
NI		nenkiake / nenkinake	nenkioke		nenkizuke	nenkizueke	nenkieke
HI	henkidake		henkioke	henkiguke			henkieke
HURA	lekidake	lekiake / lekinake	lekioke	lekiguke	lekizuke	lekizueke	lekieke
GU		genkizkiake / genkizkinake	genkizkioke		genkizkizuke	genkizkizueke	genkizkieke .
ZU	zenkizkidake		zenkizkioke	zenkizkiguke			zenkizkieke
ZUEK	zenkizkidakete		zenkizkiokete	zenkizkigukete			zenkizkiekete
HAIK	lekizkidake	lekizkiake / lekizkinake	lekizkioke	lekizkiguke	lekizkizuke	lekizkizueke	lekizkieke

ARIKETAK

Joan nenkieke inkesta bat egitera
Etor zenkizkidakete liburua ekartzera
Ahantz lekioke gogoratzen ez badiogu
Hiri horretan gerta lekizkizuke gauza
txarrak
Gerta lekizkidakeèn gertaerek ez naute
beldurtzen

I could go and make them a survey.
You could come to bring me the book.
He might forget if we don't remind him.
Bad things could happen to you in that city.

The things that might happen to me don't
frighten me.

NOR - NORI

2.7.- Potentzialezko lehenaldi urruna   Hurbil nenkiokeen   = I could have come to him

	NIRI	HIRI	HARI	GURI	ZURI	ZUEI	HAIEI
NI		nenkiakeen / nenkinakeen	nenkiokeen		nenkizukeen	nenkizuekeen	nenkiekeen
HI	henkidakeen		henkiokeen	henkigukeen			henkiekeen
HURA	zekidakeen	zekiakeen / zekinakeen	zekiokeen	zekigukeen	zekizukeen	zekizuekeen	zekiekeen
GU		genkizkiakeen / genkizkinakeen	genkizkiokeen		genkizkizukeen	genkizkizuekeen	genkizkiekeen
ZU	zenkizkidakeen		zenkizkiokeen	zenkizkigukeen			zenkizkiekeen
ZUEK	zenkizkidaketen		zenkizkioketen	zenkizkiguketen			zenkizkieketen
HAIK	zekizkidakeen	zekizkiakeen / zekizkinakeen	zekizkiokeen	zekizkigukeen	zekizkizukeen	zekizkizuekeen	zekizkiekeen

ARIKETAK

Etor zekizkigukeen, baina ez dugu haien beharrik

They could have come to us, but we don't have any need of them.

Laguntza ematera joan genkizkiokeen

We could have gone to give him help.

Arrainak berriz ere eror zekizkizuekeen uretara

The fish could have fallen into the water again (re: you).

Ondo mereziak neuzkan gerta zekizkidakeèn hainbat ezbehar

I really deserved all the problems (bad things) that could have happened to me.

NOR - NORI

2.8.- Subjuntibozko orainaldia

Hurbil nakion   = so that I will come to him.
Hurbil nakiola   = (for) me to come to him.

	NIRI	HIRI	HARI	GURI	ZURI	ZUEI	HAIEI
NI		nakian / nakinan	nakion		nakizun	nakizuen	nakien
HI	hakidan		hakion	hakigun			hakien
HURA	**dakidan**	**dakian / dakinan**	**dakion**	**dakigun**	**dakizun**	**dakizuen**	**dakien**
GU		gakizkian / gakizkinan	gakizkion		gakizkizun	gakizkizuen	gakizkien
ZU	zakizkidan		zakizkion	zakizkigun			zakizkien
ZUEK	zakizkidaten		zakizkioten	zakizkiguten			zakizkieten
HAIK	**dakizkidan**	**dakizkian / dakizkinan**	**dakizkion**	**dakizkigun**	**dakizkizun**	**dakizkizuen**	**dakizkien**

ARIKETAK

Hurbil nakiola eskatu dit
Hurbil nakion eman dit txokolatea

He has asked me to come to him.
He has given me the chocolate so that I will come to him (in order to get me to...).

Dena prestatu dugu, etxera etor za-
kizkiguten
Ardo on bat ekarri dugu, hura edateari
lot zakizkioten

We have prepared everything so that you will come to our house.
We have brought a good wine so that you will drink it. (...devote yourselves to the drinking of it).

Kontuz ibili beharko zarete, mahai gai-
nean duzuena eror ez dakizuen

You will have to be careful so that what you have on the table won't fall.

NOR - NORI

2.9.- Subjuntibozko lehenaldia

Hurbil nenkion   = so that I would come to him.

Hurbil nenkiola   = (for) me to come to him.

	NIRI	HIRI	HARI	GURI	ZURI	ZUEI	HAIEI
NI		nenkian / nenkinan	nenkion		nenkizun	nenkizuen	nenkien
HI	henkidan		henkion	henkigun			henkien
HURA	**zekidan** (lekidan)	**zekian /** **zekinan** (lekian / lekinan)	**zekion** (lekion)	**zekigun** (lekigun)	**zekizun** (lekizun)	**zekizuen** (lekizuen)	**zekien** (lekien)
GU		genkizkian / genkizkinan	genkizkion		genkizkizun	genkizkizuen	genkizkien
ZU	zenkizkidan		zenkizkion	zenkizkigun			zenkizkien
ZUEK	zenkizkidaten		zenkizkioten	zenkizkiguten			zenkizkieten
HAIK	**zekizkidan** (lekizkidan)	**zekizkian /** **zekizkinan** (lekizkian / lekizkinan)	**zekizkion** (lekizkion)	**zekizkigun** (lekizkigun)	**zekizkizun** (lekizkizun)	**zekizkizuen** (lekizkizuen)	**zekizkien** (lekizkien)

ARIKETAK

Ahaleginak egin zituen, hurbil ez nenkion   He did everything possible so that I wouldn't come to him.

Ez nizun egia esan, etor ez zenkizkidan   I didn't tell you the truth so that you wouldn't come to me (I told a lie...).

Medikua deitu zuten, aita hil ez zekien   They called the doctor so that their father wouldn't die.

Ixilik egon ginen, etxera etor ez zekizkigun   We kept quiet so that they wouldn't come to our house.

Hurbil ez nenkiola agindu zidan   He told me not to come to him.

NOR - NORI

2.10.- Inperatiboa

Hurbil bekit = he must come to me.

	NIRI	HIRI	HARI	GURI	ZURI	ZUEI	HAIEI
NI		nakia- / nakina	(nakio		nakizu	nakizue	nakie
HI	hakit		hakio	hakigu			hakie
HURA	bekit	bekik / bekin	bekio	bekigu	bekizu	bekizue	bekie
GU		gakizkia- / gakizkina	gakizkio		gakizkizu	gakizkizue	gakizkie
ZU	zakizkit		zakizkio	zakizkigu			zakizkie
ZUEK	zakizkidate		zakizkiote	zakizkigute			zakizkiete
HAIK	bekizkit	bekizkik / bekizkin	bekizkio	bekizkigu	bekizkizu	bekizkizue	bekizkie

ARIKETAK

Joan bekio laguntzera

Etor zakizkit berehala

Hurbil zakizkidate, hitzik esan gabe

Honda bekizkit ene ondasun guztiak, hau
horrela ez bada

He must go to help him.

Come to me right away.

Come to me without saying a word.

May all my belongings be lost if this isn't so.

ZER - NORK

ZER - NORK

3.1.- Indikatibozko orainaldia

Ikusi nauzu	=	you have seen me.
Ikusiko nauzu	=	you will see me.
Ikusten nauzu	=	you see me.

	NI	HI	HURA	GU	ZU	ZUEK	HAIK
NIK		haut	dut		zaitut	zaituztet	ditut
HIK	nauk / naun		duk / dun	gaituk / gaitun			dituk / ditun
HARK	nau	hau	du	gaitu	zaitu	zaituzte	ditu
GUK		haugu	dugu		zaitugu	zaituztegu	ditugu
ZUK	nauzu		duzu	gaituzu			dituzu
ZUEK	nauzue		duzue	gaituzue			dituzue
HAIEK	naute	haute	dute	gaituzte	zaituzte	zaituztete	dituzte

ARIKETAK

Nahi baduzue, gurekin eramango zaituztegu igandean	If you wish, we'll take you with us on Sunday.
Gaur goizean kalean ikusi zaituztet	I've seen you outside this morning.
Izenak ematen badizkiezue, abonatuko zaituztete	If you give them your names, they will subscribe you (to the magazine).
Aurrera joan dira, eta atzean utzi gaituzte	They've gone ahead and left us behind.
Euskal liburuak irakurtzen ditugu	We read Basque books.
Ez dugu hori apurtu behar	We aren't going to break that.
Haien esamesek guztiz samindu naute	Their gossip has made me very sad.
Haiek esandakoak guztiz mindu nau	What they have said has really hurt me.
Hurbiltzen natzaizuen bakoitzean, hizketan ikusten zaituztet	Each time I come to you, I see you speaking together.
Egunero ikusten ditut	I see them every day.
Nik ez dakit nola arraio apurtu dituzten	I don't know how in the heck they've broken them.
Ez gaituzte ikusi nahi	They don't want to see us.
Errespetatzen zaituztegu	We respect you.
Egia batere ez duzu esan	You haven't told the truth even once. (...said even one true thing).
Ez dituzu egiak esaten	You don't tell the truth.
Tontakeria asko esaten duzu	You say a lot of silly things.

ZER - NORK

3.2.- Indikatibozko lehenaldia

Ikusi ninduzun	= you saw me.
Ikusiko ninduzun	= you would have seen me.
Ikusten ninduzun	= you saw (used to see) me.

	NI	HI	HURA	GU	ZU	ZUEK	HAIK
NIK		hindudan	nuen		zintudan	zintuztedan	nituen
HIK	ninduan / nindunan		huen	gintuan / gintunan			hituen
HARK	ninduen	hinduen	zuen	gintuen	zintuen	zintuzten	zituen
GUK		hindugun	genuen		zintugun	zintuztegun	genituen
ZUK	ninduzun		zenuen	gintuzun			zenituen
ZUEK	ninduzuen		zenuten	gintuzuen			zenituzten
HAIEK	ninduten	hinduten	zuten	gintuzten	zintuzten	zintuzteten	zituzten

ARIKETAK

Atzo etxera gindoazela ikusi gintuzten	They saw us yesterday when we were going home.
Hirira ekarri zintuztegùn egunean gertatu zen hura	That happened on the day we brought you to the city.
Guztiz maite zintuen?	Did he love you very much?
Bai, bihotz bihotzez maite ninduen	Yes, he loved me with all his heart.
Ez dakit zergatik, baina gorrotatzen gintuzten	I don't know why, but they hated us.
Maite zintudan, baina zuk ez ninduzun maite	I loved you but you didn't love me.
Gorrotatzen zintuztegun, eta zuek ere gorrotatzen gintuzuen	We hated you and you hated us too.
Balio ez zutelako apurtu genituen	We tore them up because they weren't worth anything (weren't any good).
Noiz ikusi zenituzten?	When did you see them?
Atzo goizean ikusi genituen	We saw them yesterday morning.
Trukatu zenituèn seiluak oso politak ziren	The stamps you exchanged were very pretty.
Edan genuèn edaria oso gogorra zen	The drink we had was very strong.
Mapa hauk zuei ekarri nizkizuen	I brought these maps for you.
Mapa hauk zuentzat ekarri nituen	I brought these maps for you (and not for anyone else).

1
1
1

ZER - NORK

3.3.- Indikatibozko baldintza (aurrekoa)

Ikusi banindu = if he had seen me.
Ikusiko banindu = if he saw me.

	NI	HI	HURA	GU	ZU	ZUEK	HAIK
NIK		bahindut	**banu**		bazintut	bazintuztet	**banitu**
HIK	baninduk / banindun		**bahu**	bagintuk / bagintun			**bahitu**
HARK	banindu	bahindu	**balu**	bagintu	bazintu	bazintuzte	**balitu**
GUK		bahindugu	**bagenu**		bazintugu	bazintuztegu	**bagenitu**
ZUK	baninduzu		**bazenu**	bagintuzu			**bazenitu**
ZUEK	baninduzue		**bazenute**	bagintuzue			**bazenituzte**
HAIEK	banindute	bahindute	**balute**	bagintuzte	bazintuzte	bazintuztete	**balituzte**

ARIKETAK

Bakean utziko baninduzu...
Hori horrela zela jakingo banu
Oztopoak jarriko ez balitu
Goizean ikusiko ez bazintuztet
Goizean ikusi izan ez bazintuztet
Liburuak irakurriko balituzte
Irratiak entzungo bazenituzte
Telebista hainbeste ikusiko ez bazenute
Jantziak garbiagoak eramango bagenitu
Gurasoen esanak beteko balituzte

Zuen kotxean eramango bagintuzue
Hurbiltzen natzaizuenean, hizketan ikusiko ez bazintuztet
Ikasgaiak ongi ikasiko balitu, euskara asko
jakingo luke

If you left me alone (in peace)...
If I knew that was so...
If he didn't make any objections...
If I didn't see you in the morning...
If I hadn't seen you in the morning...
If they read books...
If you listened to the radio...
If you didn't watch so much television...
If we wore cleaner clothes...
If they did (fulfilled) what their parents told
them to do...

If you took us in your car...
If, when I come to you, I didn't see see you
speaking together...
If he studied the lessons well, he would know
a lot of Basque.

ZER - NORK

3.4.- Indikatibozko baldintza (ondorioa) Ikusiko nindukezu = you would see me.

	NI	HI	HURA	GU	ZU	ZUEK	HAIK
NIK		hinduket	nuke		zintuzket	zintuzketet	nituzke
HIK	nindukek / ninduken		huke	gintuzkek / gintuzken			hituzke
HARK	ninduke	hinduke	luke	gintuzke	zintuzke	zintuzkete	lituzke
GUK		hindukegu	genuke		zintuzkegu	zintuzketegu	genituzke
ZUK	nindukezu		zenuke	gintuzkezu			zenituzke
ZUEK	nindukezue		zenukete	gintuzkezue			zenituzkete
HAIEK	nindukete	hindukete	lukete	gintuzkete	zintuzkete	zintuzketete	lituzkete

ARIKETAK

Posible balitz, egingo nuke
Ahal izango bagenu, ekarriko genituzke
Zer egin behar nuke, ni errespetatua iza-
teko?
Ekarriko bazintuztet, zer egingo zenukete?
Gure arrazoiak ez lituzkete kontuan har-
tuko
Hori horrela ez dela jakin behar zenuke
Gehiago ikasi behar zenukete
Etorriko ez banintz ez nindukezu ikusiko
Beste edozeinek hartuko zintuzkete
Hori ikusiko balute, nolako aurpegiak ipi-
niko lituzkete!
Entzun egingo nindukete, eta konbentzi-
tuko nituzke
Ba dirudi Jainkoak nire errua zigortu nahi
lukeela
Arraultzeak hobe frijitu behar zenituzke

If it were possible, I'd do it.
We'd bring them if we could.
What would I have to do in order to be res-
pected?
If I brought you, what would you do?
They wouldn't take our reasons into account.

You should know that it's not like that.
You should study more.
If I didn't come, you wouldn't see me.
Anyone else would take you.
If they saw that, what faces they would
make!
They would hear me an I would convince
them.
It seems as though God wanted to punish (me
for) my transgression.
You should fry the eggs better.

ZER - NORK

3.5.- Potentzialezko orainaldia

Ikus nazake = he can/may see me.

	NI	HI	HURA	GU	ZU	ZUEK	HAIK
NIK		hazaket	dezaket		zaitzaket	zaitzaketet	ditzaket
HIK	nazakek / nazaken		dezakek / dezaken	gaitzakek / gaitzaken			ditzakek / ditzaken
HARK	nazake	hazake	dezake	gaitzake	zaitzake	zaitzakete	ditzake
GUK		hazakegu	dezakegu		zaitzakegu	zaitzaketegu	ditzakegu
ZUK	nazakezu		dezakezu	gaitzakezu			ditzakezu
ZUEK	nazakezue		dezakezue	gaitzakezue			ditzakezue
HAIEK	nazakete	hazakete	dezakete	gaitzakete	zaitzakete	zaitzaketete	ditzakete

ARIKETAK

Eraman nazakezu, baina astiro	You can take me, but (drive) slowly.
Zer egin dezaket?	What can I do?
Fitxak egin ditzakezu	You can do exercises.
Kutxa horretan gorde ditzakezu boligrafoak	You can put the ball-point pens in that box.
Bihar ikus dezakezu teatroan	Tomorrow you can see him at the theater.
Zeure besoetan har nazakezu	You can take me in yours arms.
Nahi badut, bazter eraz zaitzaket	If I wish, I can make you feel left out.
Zer egin dezakegu orain?	What can we do now?
Ezin dezakezue ezer egin	You can't do anything.
Gehiago jan dezakete	They can eat more.
Apur ditzakegu paper zahar hauk?	Can we tear up these old papers?
Ez, ezin ditzakezue apur	No, you can't tear them up.
Ezin nazakezue bakarrik utz	You can't leave me by myself.
Ezin zaitzakegu bakarrik utz	We can't leave you by yourself.
Oso erraz egin dezaket hori	I can do that quite easily.

ZER - NORK

3.8.- Subjuntibozko orainaldia

Ikus nazan = so that he can/will see me.
Ikus nazala = that he should see me
(for) him to see me.

	NI	HI	HURA	GU	ZU	ZUEK	HAIK
NIK		hazadan	**dezadan**		zaitzadan	zaitzatedan	**ditzadan**
HIK	nazaan / nazanan		**dezaan / dezanan**	gaitzaan / gaitzanan			**ditzaan/ ditzanan**
HARK	nazan	hazan	**dezan**	gaitzan	zaitzan	zaitzaten	**ditzan**
GUK		hazagun	**dezagun**		zaitzagun	zaitzategun	**ditzagun**
ZUK	nazazun		**dezazun**	gaitzazun			**ditzazun**
ZUEK	nazazuen		**dezazuen**	gaitzazuen			**ditzazuen**
HAIEK	nazaten	hazaten	**dezaten**	gaitzaten	zaitzaten	zaitzateten	**ditzaten**

ARIKETAK

Kapataz berria ekarri diete, lan gehiago egin dezaten	They've brought them a new foreman so that they will work harder.
Soldata jaso digute, greba egin ez dezagun	They've raised our salary so we won't go on strike.
Etor zaitez honantz, hobe ikus zaitzagun	Come closer so we can see you better.
Papera erosi diet, ikastolarako fitxak egin ditzaten	I've bought them the paper so they can do exercises for school.
Ezkutatu gara, ikus ez gaitzazuen	We are hiding so you won't see us.
Lan egingo dugu, euskarak gora egin dezan	We will work (hard) so that the Basque language will rise.
Amak esan dit sal ditzagula liburuok	Mother has told me that we should sell these books.
Barka zaitzategula eskatu digute	They've asked us to forgive you.

ZER - NORK

3.7.- Potentzialezko lehenaldi urruna   Ikus nintzakeen   = he could have seen me.

	NI	HI	HURA	GU	ZU	ZUEK	HAIK
NIK		hintzakedan	**nezakeen**		zintzakedan	zintzaketedan	**nitzakeen**
HIK	nintzakean / nintzakenan		**hezakeen**	gintzakean / gintzakenan			**hitzakeen**
HARK	nintzakeen	hintzakeen	**zezakeen**	gintzakeen	zintzakeen	zintzaketen	**zitzakeen**
GUK		hintzakegun	**genezakeen**		zintzakegun	zintzaketegun	**genitzakeen**
ZUK	nintzakezun		**zenezakeen**	gintzakezun			**zenitzakeen**
ZUEK	nintzakezuen		**zenezaketen**	gintzakezuen			**zenitzaketen**
HAIEK	nintzaketen	hintzaketen	**zezaketen**	gintzaketen	zintzaketen	zintzaketeten	**zitzaketen**

ARIKETAK

Lehen genuèn kamioiak hogei tonelada eraman zitzakeen	The truck we had before could have carried 20 tons.
Eskatuko bazenit, egin nezakeen	If you had asked me to, I could have done it.
Egin zezakeen, baina ez zuen nahi izan	He could have done it, but he didn't want to.
Kotxe berrian eraman zintzakegun	We could have taken you in the new car.
Ekar nintzakezuen eskatu banizue?	Would you have been able to bring me, if I had asked you to?
Ezin zezaketen pisu hori altxa	They wouldn't have been able to lift that weight.
Mailuak egin genitzakeen, burdin nahikoa ukan bagenu	We would have been able to make the hammers if we had had enough iron.
Atzokoa esan zenezaketen, utziko bali- zuete	You could have told them about (what happened) yesterday if they had let you.
Hori litzateke ongien egin zenezaketena	That would be the best thing you could have done.
Egutegia begira zenezakeen	You could have looked at the calendar.
Lan egin zezaketen	They could have worked.

ZER - NORK

3.6.- Potentzialezko lehenaldia

Ikus nintzake = he could/might see me.

	NI	HI	HURA	GU	ZU	ZUEK	HAIK
NIK		hintzaket	**nezake**		zintzaket	zintzaketet	**nitzake**
HIK	nintzakek / nintzaken		**hezake**	gintzakek / gintzaken			**hitzake**
HARK	nintzake	hintzake	**lezake**	gintzake	zintzake	zintzakete	**litzake**
GUK		hintzakegu	**genezake**		zintzakegu	zintzaketegu	**genitzake**
ZUK	nintzakezu		**zenezake**	gintzakezu			**zenitzake**
ZUEK	nintzakezue		**zenezakete**	gintzakezue			**zenitzakete**
HAIEK	nintzakete	hintzakete	**lezakete**	gintzakete	zintzakete	zintzaketete	**litzakete**

ARIKETAK

Hari batek harengana eraman gintzake

A thread could lead us to him.

Har nintzakezu zeure kotxean?

Could you take me in your car?

Ezin zintzaket har, dena beterik dagoelako

I wouldn't be able to take you because it's all full.

Har nezake horietariko bat?

Could I take one of those?

Ezin zenitzake har zuhaitzetako gereziak

You wouldn't be able to get the cherries in the trees.

Ezin lezake koadroa pinta

He wouldn't be able to paint the picture.

Ezin litzake koadroak pinta

He wouldn't be able to paint the pictures.

Nahi lituzketen txori guztiak ekar litzakete

They would be able to take all the birds they wanted.

Zure anaiak zinema horretako filmeak ikus litzake

Your brother could see the movies (they show) in that theater.

Fabrikako erramintak eraman zenitzakete

You could take the factory tools.

Denok elkarrekin bazkal genezake

We could all have lunch together.

Gauza asko egin genezake

We could do many things.

Ogiak egin genitzake

We could make bread.

ZER - NORK

3.9.- Subjuntibozko lehenaldia

Ikus nintzan = so that he could/would see me.
Ikus nintzala = that he should see me
(for) him to see me.

	NI	HI	HURA	GU	ZU	ZUEK	HAIK
NIK		hintzadan	**nezan**		zintzadan	zintzatedan	**nitzan**
HIK	nintzaan / nintzanan		**hezan**	gintzaan / gintzanan			**hitzan**
HARK	nintzan	hintzan	**zezan / lezan**	gintzan	zintzan	zintzaten	**zitzan / litzan**
GUK		hintzagun	**genezan**		zintzagun	zintzategun	**genitzan**
ZUK	nintzazun		**zenezan**	gintzazun			**zenitzan**
ZUEK	nintzazuen		**zenezaten**	gintzazuen			**zenitzaten**
HAIEK	nintzaten	hintzaten	**zezaten / lezaten**	gintzaten	zintzaten	zintzateten	**zitzaten / litzaten**

ARIKETAK

Sorora eraman gintuen lan egin genezan
Lan egin genezala esan ziguten
Zuengana joan ginen, ikus zintzategun

Oinez joan nintzen, bidean har nintza-
zuen
Har nintzazuela eskatu nizuen
Zerbait ekar zezatela agindu zizueten

He took us to the field so we would work.
They told us to work.
We went to you so we could see you.

I went on foot so you could pick me up.

I asked you to pick me up.
They ordered you to get them to bring something.

ZER - NORK

3.10.- Inperatiboa

Ikus nazazu   = see me/you must see me.

	NI	HI	HURA	GU	ZU	ZUEK	HAIK
NIK		hazat			zaitzat	zaitzatet	
HIK	nazak / nazan		**ezak / ezan**	gaitzak / gaitzan			**itzak / itzan**
HARK	naza	haza	**beza**	gaitza	zaitza	zaitzate	**bitza**
GUK		hazazu			zaitzagu	zaitzategu	
ZUK	nazazu		**ezazu**	gaitzazu			**itzazu**
ZUEK	nazazue		**ezazue**	gaitzazue			**itzazue**
HAIEK	nazate	hazate	**bezate**	gaitzate	zaitzate	zaitzatete	**bitzate**

ARIKETAK

Ikus beza nola dagoen bide hori	He must see what that road is like.
Eraman gaitzazu kotxean	Take us in the car.
Ez bezate horrelakorik egin	They mustn't do anything like that.
Har bitza lapitzak	He must pick up the pencils.
Utz beza botila	He must put the bottle down.
Har gaitzazu garen bezala	Take us as we are.
Ikus gaitzazue nola gauden	See how we are.

ZER - NORI - NORK

ZER - NORI - NORK

4.1.a.- Indikatibozko orainaldia

Eman diot   = I've given it to him.
Emango diot   = I'll give it to him.
Ematen diot   = I give it to him.

	NIRI	HIRI	HARI	GURI	ZURI	ZUEI	HAIEI
NIK		diat / dinat	diot		dizut	dizuet	diet
HIK	didak / didan		diok / dion	diguk / digun			diek / dien
HARK	dit	dik / din	dio	digu	dizu	dizue	die
GUK		diagu / dinagu	diogu		dizugu	dizuegu	diegu
ZUK	didazu		diozu	diguzu			diezu
ZUEK	didazue		diozue	diguzue			diezue
HAIEK	didate	diate / dinate	diote	digute	dizute	dizuete	diete

ARIKETAK

Egin behar dutena esan diete

Ostiko bat eman dio

Apur bat besterik ez diozu eman

Atzo eskatu geniona ekarri digu

Ez dizut ezer gehiagorik esango

Badaezpadan ez diot ezer esan

Ez dakit zergatik, baina ez diguzue kasurik egiten

Hau ekarri dizuegu, gurekin haserre ez zaitezten

Ez ditugu gehiagotan deituko

Txerrikeria bat egin digute

Ez didazue horrelakorik esan

Gabonetan jostailu asko ekarri diote

Ez dit egia azaldu

Ez diot konfidantzarik

Irakasleari begiramena zor diozue

Irakasleari zor diozuen begiramena

They've told them what they must do.

He has kicked him (given him a kick).

You've only given him a little.

He's brought us what we asked for yesterday.

I won't tell you anything more.

Just in case, I haven't told him anything.

I don't know why, but you don't pay any attention to us.

We've brought you this so you won't get angry at us.

We won't call them any more.

They've played a dirty trick on us.

You haven't told me anything like that.

They brought him a lot of presents for Christmas.

He hasn't explained (told) me the truth.

I haven't any confidence in him.

You owe respect to the teacher.

The respect that you owe the teacher...

ZER - NORI - NORK

4.1.b.- Indikatibozko orainaldia

Eman dizkiot	=	I've given them to him.
Emango dizkiot	=	I'll give them to him.
Ematen dizkiot	=	I give them to him.

	NIRI	HIRI	HARI	GURI	ZURI	ZUEI	HAIEI
NIK		dizkiat / dizkinat	dizkiot		dizkizut	dizkizuet	dizkiet
HIK	dizkidak / dizkidan		dizkiok / dizkion	dizkiguk / dizkigun			dizkiek / dizkien
HARK	dizkit	dizkik / dizkin	dizkio	dizkigu	dizkizu	dizkizue	dizkie
GUK		dizkiagu / dizkinagu	dizkiogu		dizkizugu	dizkizuegu	dizkiegu
ZUK	dizkidazu		dizkiozu	dizkiguzu			dizkiezu
ZUEK	dizkidazue		dizkiozue	dizkiguzue			dizkiezue
HAIEK	dizkidate	dizkiate / dizkinate	dizkiote	dizkigute	dizkizute	dizkizuete	dizkiete

ARIKETAK

Azaldu dizkidazun ideiak ongi ikusten ditut	I like the ideas you have explained to me.
Ikusi dizkiguzuen kutxak ez ziren gureak	The boxes you've seen weren't ours.
Eskatutako dokumentuak ekarri dizkizuegu	We've brought you the petitioned documents.
Eman al dizkiozu? Bai, eman dizkiot	Have you given them to him? Yes, I've given them to him.
Ixiltzen ez bazara, bi belarrondoko eman-go dizkizut	I'll give you two smacks if you're not quiet.
Gauza politak ekarri dizkiet	I've brought them beautiful things.
Ez dakizu nolako gauza politak ekarri dizkiedan	You don't know what beautiful things I've brought them.
Jostailuak eman dizkit	He has given me toys.
Eman dizkidan jostailuak	The toys he has given me...
Aulkiak konpondu dizkio	He fixed the chairs for him.
Konpondu dizkion aulkiak	The chairs he fixed for him...
Eskatu dizueguna ez da guretzat	What we have asked you for is not for us.

ZER - NORI - NORK

4.2.a.- Indikatibozko lehenaldia

Eman nion	= I gave it to him.
Emango nion	= I would have given it to him.
Ematen nion	= I was giving it to him.

	NIRI	HIRI	HARI	GURI	ZURI	ZUEI	HAIEI
NIK		nian / ninan	nion		nizun	nizuen	nien
HIK	hidan		hion	higun			hien
HARK	zidan	zian / zinan	zion	zigun	zizun	zizuen	zien
GUK		genian / geninan	genion		genizun	genizuen	genien
ZUK	zenidan		zenion	zenigun			zenien
ZUEK	zenidaten		zenioten	zeniguten			zenieten
HAIEK	zidaten	ziaten/zinaten	zioten	ziguten	zizuten	zizueten	zieten

ARIKETAK

Hark esandakoak bost axola zidan	What he told me didn't matter to me.
Zure anaiari eman nion	I gave it to your brother.
Zure anaiari eman niòn egutegia	The calendar that I gave your brother...
Atzo bidali nizun eskatu zenidàn telegrama	Yesterday I sent you the telegram you asked me for.
Bazkari on bat eskaini zieten	They gave them a good lunch.
Hori egingo banu, inozo bat naizela esango zenidaten	If I did that, you would tell me I'm a fool.
Gezurra esan zeniguten	You told us a lie.
Egia esan genizuen	We told you the truth.
Erregalu on bat eman zigun	He gave us a good present.
Eman zigùn erregalu ona	The good present he gave us...
Erregalu on bat emango zigun	He would have given us a good present.
Emango zigùn erregalu ona	The good present he would have given us...

ZER - NORI - NORK

4.2.b.- Indikatibozko lehenaldia

Eman nizkion = I gave them to him.
Emango nizkion = I would have given them to him.
Ematen nizkion = I was giving them to him.

	NIRI	HIRI	HARI	GURI	ZURI	ZUEI	HAIEI
NIK		nizkian / nizkinan	nizkion		nizkizun	nizkizuen	nizkien
HIK	hizkidan	·	hizkion	hizkigun			hizkien
HARK	zizkidan	zizkian / zizkinan	zizkion	zizkigun	zizkizun	zizkizuen	zizkien
GUK	·	genizkian / genizkinan	genizkion		genizkizun	genizkizuen	genizkien
ZUK	zenizkidan		zenizkion	zenizkigun			zenizkien
ZUEK	zenizkidaten		zenizkioten	zenizkiguten			zenizkieten
HAIEK	zizkidaten	zizkiaten / zizkinaten	zizkioten	zizkiguten	zizkizuten	zizkizueten	zizkieten

ARIKETAK

Zure anaiari eman nizkiòn kromoak zuretzat ziren

The cards I gave your brother were for you.

Zertarako dira eman zenizkigutèn fitxeroak?

What are the filing cabinets you gave us for?

Zuentzat ekarri genituen

We brought them for you.

Kontatu zizkigunak entzunda, ez dakit zer pentsa

(Now that I've) heard the things he told us, I don't know what to think.

Onak zirelakoan ekarri genizkizun

We brought them for you thinking they were good.

Ez esan gero ekarri ez nizkiola

Don't say later that I didn't bring them to him.

Ezin dizut esan ekarri zizkidala

I can't say he brought them to me.

Ekarri nizkizuela pentsatu zenuten

You thought I brought them to you.

Gurpilak puztu zizkioten

They filled the tires with air for him.

Despuztu zizkiotèn gurpilak

The flat tires...

Telebistatik entzun nizkionak gezur biribilak ziren

The things I heard him say on TV were big fat lies.

Eman zizkigutèn txanponak faltsoak ziren

The coins they gave us were counterfeit.

ZER - NORI - NORK

4.3.a.- Indikatibozko baldintza (aurrekoa)

Eman banio   = if I had given it to him.
Emango banio = if I gave it to him.

	NIRI	HIRI	HARI	GURI	ZURI	ZUEI	HAIEI
NIK		banik / banin	banio		banizu	banizue	banie
HIK	bahit		bahio	bahigu			bahie
HARK	balit	balik / balin	balio	baligu	balizu	balizue	balie
GUK		bagenik / bagenin	bagenio		bagenizu	bagenizue	bagenie
ZUK	bazenit		bazenio	bazenigu			bazenie
ZUEK	bazenidate		bazeniote	bazenigute			bazeniete
HAIEK	balidate	baliate / balinate	baliote	baligute	balizute	balizuete	baliete

ARIKETAK

Afaria goizago emango bagenie, hobe egingo lukete lo	If we gave them dinner earlier, they'd sleep better.
Afaltzen arinago emango bazenio, loak arinago hartuko luke	If you gave him his dinner earlier, he'd go to sleep sooner (sleep would catch him).
Bere luma utziko balit, neurea emango nioke	If he lent me his pen, I'd give him mine.
Laguntza gehiago emango bazeniote, gehiago jakingo luke	If you gave him more help, he'd know more.
Liburua arinago ekarriko balidate, gehiago ikasiko nuke	If they brought me the book sooner, I'd learn more.
Nolako baserria zuen ikusiko bazenio!	If you could only see (if you saw) what a farm he had.
Liburua utziko banio, ez lidake bihurtuko	If I lent him the book he wouldn't give it back to me.
Hobe kasurik egingo ez bazenio	It would be better if you didn't pay any attention to him.
Arreta gehiago bazenit, denda hobe zuzenduko genuke	If you paid more attention to me, we would manage the store better.
Lepoa emango ez baligute, indartsuagoak ginateke	If they didn't turn their backs on us, we'd be stronger.
Euskararen batasunari lagunduko bagenio, gure hizkuntza gehiago indartuko litzateke	If we helped in the unification of Basque, our language would be fortified.

ZER - NORI - NORK

4.3.b.- Indikatibozko baldintza (aurrekoa)

Eman banizkio = if I had given them to him.
Emango banizkio = if I gave them to him.

	NIRI	HIRI	HARI	GURI	ZURI	ZUEI	HAIEI
NIK		banizkik / banizkin	banizkio		banizkizu	banizkizue	banizkie
HIK	bahizkit		bahizkio	bahizkigu			bahizkie
HARK	balizkit	balizkik / balizkin	balizkio	balizkigu	balizkizu	balizkizue	balizkie
GUK		bagenizkik / bagenizkin	bagenizkio		bagenizkizu	bagenizkizue	bagenizkie
ZUK	bazenizkit		bazenizkio	bazenizkigu			bazenizkie
ZUEK	bazenizkidate		bazenizkiote	bazenizkigute			bazenizkiete
HAIEK	balizkidate	balizkiate / balizkinate	balizkiote	balizkigute	balizkizute	balizkizuete	balizkiete

ARIKETAK

Sagarrak ekarriko balizkit, pozik jango nituzke
If he brought me apples I'd eat them happily.

Jateko arraultzeak emango bazenizkiete, hobe jango lukete
If you gave them eggs to eat, they would eat better.

Azaldu zizkidanak esango banizkizu, ikaratu egingo zinateke
If I told you the things he explained to me, you'd be shocked.

Zuri egin balizkizu, besterik esango zenuke
If he had done them to you, you'd speak differently.

Haik bezalako koadroak pintatuko balizkigu, orman ezarriko genituzke
If he painted us pictures like that, we'd hang them on the wall.

Ardo botilak eramango banizkio, berehala edango lituzke
If I took him the bottles of wine, he'd drink them right away.

Gaurko egunkariak ekarriko bazenizkit, asko eskertuko nizuke
If you brought me today's newspapers, I'd be most grateful to you.

Hizlariei entzungo bazeniete, gauza jakingarriak jasoko zenituzkete
If you listened to the speakers, you would catch (pick up) some interesting ideas.

Eroriko balitzait, jasoko nuke
If I dropped it, I would pick it up.

ZER - NORI - NORK

4.4.a.- Indikatibozko baldintza (ondorioa)   Emango nioke   = I would give it to him.

	NIRI	HIRI	HARI	GURI	ZURI	ZUEI	HAIEI
NIK		niake / ninake	nioke		nizuke	nizueke	nieke
HIK	hidake		hioke	higuke			hieke
HARK	lidake	liake / linake	lioke	liguke	lizuke	lizueke	lieke
GUK		geniake / geninake	genioke		genizuke	genizueke	genieke
ZUK	zenidake		zenioke	zeniguke			zenieke
ZUEK	zenidakete		zeniokete	zenigukete			zeniekete
HAIEK	lidakete	liakete / linakete	liokete	ligukete	lizukete	lizuekete	liekete

ARIKETAK

Ezkutuan esango balidate, hobe litzateke

Emango lioke erantzun bat

Zerbait eskatuko bazenit, emango nizuke

Ikusiko banu, erloju berria erakutsiko nioke

Zer ordainduko liguke lan hori egingo bagenio?

Galdera hori egingo bagenio, erantzungo liguke

Onak izango bagina, gozoki bana emango zenigukete

Hurbilduko balitzait, musu bat emango nioke

Gaixotuko balitz, medikuari etor ledin eskatuko nioke

Etorriko bazinete, sari eder bat emango genizueke

If they told it to me in secret, it would be better.

He would give him an answer.

If you asked me for something, I'd give it to you.

If I saw him, I'd show him the new clock.

What would he pay us if we did that job?

If we asked him that question, he'd answer us.

If we were good, you would give us each a treat.

If he came to me, I'd give him a kiss.

If he got sick, I'd ask the doctor to come.

If you came, we'd give you a nice surprise.

ZER - NORI - NORK

4.4.b.- Indikatibozko baldintza (ondorioa)   Emango nizkioke = I'd give them to him.

	NIRI	HIRI	HARI	GURI	ZURI	ZUEI	HAIEI
NIK		nizkiake / nizkinake	nizkioke		nizkizuke	nizkizueke	nizkieke
HIK	hizkidake		hizkioke	hizkiguke			hizkieke
HARK	lizkidake	lizkiake / lizkinake	lizkioke	lizkiguke	lizkizuke	lizkizueke	lizkieke
GUK		genizkiake / genizkinake	genizkioke		genizkizuke	genizkizueke	genizkieke
ZUK	zenizkidake		zenizkioke	zenizkiguke			zenizkieke
ZUEK	zenizkidakete		zenizkiokete	zenizkigukete			zenizkiekete
HAIEK	lizkidakete	lizkiakete / lizkinakete	lizkiokete	lizkigukete	lizkizukete	lizkizuekete	lizkiekete

ARIKETAK

Eskatuko banizu, atzo ekarritako aldizkariak emango zenizkieke	If I asked you to, you would give them the magazines that were brought yesterday.
Berandu izango ez balitz, idazlanak idatziko nizkioke	If it weren't (so) late, I'd write him the articles.
Argiago idatziak baleude, aldizkari horik irakurriko nizkizuke	If they were written more clearly, I'd read you those magazines.
Behar den bezala ordainduko baligute, kamioiak kargatuko genizkieke	If they paid us as they should, we'd load the trucks for them.
Materialik gabe ezin egin nizkizueke bulegoko lanak	Without materials, I wouldn't be able to do the office work for you.
Apurtuko balizkit, ez nizkizuke besteak erosiko	If he broke them, I wouldn't buy you the others.
Txanponak emango bazenizkigu, madariak emango genizkizuke	If you gave us the coins, we'd give you the pears.
Harriak kenduko bazenizkigute, sariak banatuko genizkizueke	If you got rid of the rocks for us, we'd give you each a present.
Ondo portatuko balitz, zertzu emango zenizkioke?	If he behaved well, what would you give him?
Fruituak emango nizkioke	I'd give him fruit.

ZER - NORI - NORK

4.5.a.- Potentzialezko orainaldia

Eman diezaioket   = I can give it to him.

	NIRI	HIRI	HARI	GURI	ZURI	ZUEI	HAIEI
NIK		diezaaket / diezanaket	diezaioket		diezazuket	diezazueket	diezaieket
HIK	diezadakek / diezadaken		diezaiokek / diezaioken	diezagukek / diezaguken			diezaiekek / diezaieken
HARK	diezadake	diezaake / diezanake	diezaioke	diezaguke	diezazuke	diezazueke	diezaieke
GUK		diezaakegu / diezanakegu	diezaiokegu		diezazukegu	diezazuekegu	diezaiekegu
ZUK	diezadakezu		diezaiokezu	diezagukezu			diezaiekezu
ZUEK	diezadakezue		diezaiokezue	diezagukezue			diezaiekezue
HAIEK	diezadakete	diezaakete / diezanakete	diezaiokete	diezagukete	diezazukete	diezazuekete	diezaiekete

ARIKETAK

Nahi baduzu, liburu hau utzi diezazuket irakurtzeko	If you want, I can lend you this book to read.
Eman diezadakezu zigarro bat?	Can you give me a cigarette?
Ez dut erretzen eta, beraz, ezin diezazuket zigarro bat eman	I don't smoke, and so I can't give you a cigarette.
Eskatu dizun janaria ekar diezaiokezu	You can take him the food he asked you for.
Bere lana ordain diezaiokezu arotzari	You can pay the carpenter for his work.
Ikatza eska diezaiekezue	You can ask them for coal.
Konpon al diezadakezue automobila?	Can you fix the car for me?
Ez, ezin diezazukegu automobila konpon	No, we can't fix the car for you.
Ipin al diezaiekezu telebista?	Can you turn the TV on for them?
Ez, ezin diezaieket telebista ipin	No, I can't turn the TV on for them.
Eman al diezadakezu afaria?	Can you give me dinner?
Ez, ezin diezazuket afaria eman	No, I can't give you dinner.
Dei egin al diezazuekete telefonoz?	Can they call you on the telephone?
Ez, ezin diezazagukete dei egin telefonoz	No, they can't phone us.
Ekar diezazuekegu tornua?	Can we bring you the lathe?
Ez, ezin diezazagukezue tornua ekar	No, you can't bring us the lathe.
Eman diezaioket. Har diezaieket	I can give it to him. I can catch them.
Donostiatik idatz diezadakezue	You can write me from San Sebastian.

147

ZER - NORI - NORK

4.5.b.- Potentzialezko orainaldia   Eman diezazkioket = I can give them to him.

	NIRI	HIRI	HARI	GURI	ZURI	ZUEI	HAIEI
NIK		diezazkiaket / diezazkinaket	diezazkioket		diezazkizuket	diezazkizueket	diezazkieket
HIK	diezazkidakek / diezazkidaken		diezazkiokek / diezazkioken	diezazkigukek / diezazkiguken			diezazkiekek / diezazkieken
HARK	diezazkidake	diezazkiake / diezazkinake	diezazkioke	diezazkiguke	diezazkizuke	diezazkizueke	diezazkieke
GUK		diezazkiakegu / diezazkinakegu	diezazkiokegu		diezazkizukegu	diezazkizuekegu	diezazkiekegu
ZUK	diezazkidakezu		diezazkiokezu	diezazkigukezu			diezazkiekezu
ZUEK	diezazkidakezue		diezazkiokezue	diezazkigukezue			diezazkiekezue
HAIEK	diezazkidakete	diezazkiakete / diezazkinakete	diezazkiokete	diezazkigukete	diezazkizukete	diezazkizuekete	diezazkiekete

ARIKETAK

Eros diezazkizueket banana horik?	Can I buy you those bananas?
Ez, ezin eros diezazkidakezue banana horik	No, you can't buy me those bananas.
Ekar diezazkidakete ardo botilak?	Can they bring me the wine bottles?
Ez, ezin ekar diezazkizukete ardo botilak	No, they can't bring you the wine bottles.
Aldizkari horik Baionan lor diezazkidakezue	You can get those magazines for me in Bayona.
Iruinean ere lor diezazkigukezue	You can also get them for us in Pamplona.
Eman diezazkiokegu albumak?	Can we give him the albums?
Ez, ezin eman diezazkiokezue albumak	No, you can't give him the albums.
Ez dakit lur honetan nolako gertaerak itxadon diezazkidaketen	I don't know what the future has in store for me in this land (what events are waiting for me).
Eman diezazkidake	He can give them to me.
Nolako gauzak eman diezazkidakeen!	He can give me such (amazing) things!
Nolako gauzak esan diezazkiokedan!	I can tell him such (surprising) things!
Esan diezazkiokedan gauzak	The things I can tell him.
Azal diezazkiokedan gauzak kontaezinak dira	The things that I can explain to him are innumerable.
Sagarra eros diezazuket. Sagarrak eros diezazkizuket. Sagar asko eros diezazuket	I can buy you the apple. I can buy you the apples. I can buy you many apples.

ZER - NORI - NORK

4.6.a. Potentzialezko lehenaldia Eman nezaioke   = I could give it to him.

	NIRI	HIRI	HARI	GURI	ZURI	ZUEI	HAIEI
NIK		niezaake / niezanake	niezaioke		niezazuke	niezazueke	niezaieke
HIK	hiezadake		hiezaioke	hiezaguke			hiezaieke
HARK	liezadake	liezaake / liezanake	liezaioke	liezaguke	liezazuke	liezazueke	liezaieke
GUK		geniezaake / geniezanake	geniezaioke		geniezazuke	geniezazueke	geniezaieke
ZUK	zeniezadake		zeniezaioke	zeniezaguke			zeniezaieke
ZUEK	zeniezadakete		zeniezaiokete	zeniezagukete			zeniezaiekete
HAIEK	liezadakete	liezaakete / liezanakete	liezaiokete	liezagukete	liezazukete	liezazuekete	liezaiekete

ARIKETAK

Zer egin niezaioke, nahi ez badu?

Ezin liezaioke etxe hori eros
Ekar geniezazukeèn dokumentuak ez luke deus balioko
Alda zeniezadake jantzi hau?
Dirua truka zenezakete
Ezin liezagukete esan ordua
Zuk ekarritako koadroa eman niezaioke
Gorde zeniezadake kotxea zeure garajean?
Min egin liezagukete
Postaz bidal geniezaioke pakete hori
Kartera hori eman geniezazueke
Esne botila apur liezadake
Esne botila apur liezadakete
Apur liezadakeen botila ona da
Ekar liezaguketen gozokia
Eman niezaiokeèn musua
Ezin ekar zeniezadakeèn ogia
Euskal erromantze bat dei geniezaioke gaskoinari

What can I do to him (about that) if he doesn't want to?
He couldn't buy that house from him.
The document we could bring you wouldn't be worth anything.
Could you exchange this suit for me?
You could exchange the money.
They couldn't tell us the time.
I could give him the picture you brought.
Could you keep my car in your garage?
They could hurt us.
We could send them that package by mail.
We could give you that briefcase.
He could/might break the bottle of milk.
They might break the bottle of milk.
The bottle they might break is a good one.
The treat they might bring us...
The kiss I might give him...
The bread you couldn't bring me...
We could call Gascon a Romance (form of) Basque.

ZER - NORI - NORK

4.6.b.- Potentzialezko lehenaldia

Eman niezazkioke = I could give them to him.

	NIRI	HIRI	HARI	GURI	ZURI	ZUEI	HAIEI
NIK		niezazkiake / niezazkinake	niezazkioke	.	niezazkizuke	niezazkizueke	niezazkieke
HIK	hiezazkidake		hiezazkioke	hiezazkiguke			hiezazkieke
HARK	liezazkidake	liezazkiake / liezazkinake	liezazkioke.	liezazkiguke	liezazkizuke	liezazkizueke	liezazkieke
GUK		geniezazkiake/ geniezazkinake	geniezazkioke		geniezazkizuke	geniezazkizueke	geniezazkieke
ZUK	zeniezazkidake		zeniezazkioke	zeniezazkiguke			zeniezazkieke
ZUEK	zeniezazkidakete		zeniezazkiokete	zeniezazkigukete			zeniezazkiekete
HAIEK	liezazkidakete	liezazkiakete / liezazkinakete	liezazkiokete	liezazkigukete	liezazkizukete	liezazkizuekete	liezazkiekete

ARIKETAK

Pinuak eros niezazkioke aulkiak egiteko | I might buy the pinetrees from him to make chairs.

Jostailu horik konpon geniezazkizuke | We could fix those toys for you.

Gaurko egunkariak irakur zeniezazkidake | You could read me today's newspapers.

Sal geniezazkieke haiei olio bidoiak? | Could we sell them the cans of (cooking) oil.

Ez, ezin sal zeniezazkiekete | No, you couldn't sell them to them.

Ekar liezazkigukete idazmakinak? | Could they bring us the typewriters?

Ez, ezin ekar liezazkizuekete | No, they couldn't bring them to you.

Ekar liezazkiguketen idazmakinak | The typewriters they could bring us...

Eman niezazkiokeèn gaztak | The cheese I could give them...

Eman zeniezazkiguke gaurko ogiak? | Could you give us today's loaves of bread?

Ez, ezin eman niezazkizueke gaurko ogiak | No, I couldn't give you today's bread.

Gogoan har horrek ekar liezazkizukeèn abantailak | Remember the advantages that that could bring you.

ZER - NORI - NORK

4.7.a.- Potentzialezko lehenaldi urruna   Eman niezaiokeen   =I could have given it to him.

	NIRI	HIRI	HARI	GURI	ZURI	ZUEI	HAIEI
NIK		niezaakeen / niezanakeen	niezaiokeen		niezazukeen	niezazuekeen	niezaiekeen
HIK	hiezadakeen		hiezaiokeen	hiezagukeen			hiezaiekeen
HARK	ziezadakeen	ziezaakeen / ziezanakeen	ziezaiokeen	ziezagukeen	ziezazukeen	ziezazuekeen	ziezaiekeen
GUK		geniezaakeen/ geniezanakeen	geniezaiokeen		geniezazukeen	geniezazuekeen	geniezaiekeen
ZUK	zeniezadakeen		zeniezaiokeen	zeniezagukeen			zeniezaiekeen
ZUEK	zeniezadaketen		zeniezaioketen	zeniezaguketen			zeniezaieketen
HAIEK	ziezadaketen	ziezaaketen / ziezanaketen	ziezaioketen	ziezaguketen	ziezazuketen	ziezazueketen	ziezaieketen

ARIKETAK

Asma zeniezagukeèn ipuinak ez luke ba-
liorik izango

Ekar ziezaiokeèn magnetofoia kanpotik
ekarria litzateke

Eman geniezaiokeèn aldizkaria euskalduna
litzateke

Idatz niezaiekeèn lana ez litzateke ona
izango

Konta ziezaguketèn esamesa gezurra litzateke

The story you could have invented for us wouldn't have been any good.

The tape recorder he could have brought him would be brought from abroad.

The magazine we could have given him would be Basque.

The work I could have written for them wouldn't be good.

The rumor they could have told us would be a lie.

ZER - NORI - NORK

4.7.b.- Potentzialezko lehenaldi urruna   Eman niezazkiokeen = I could have given them to him.

	NIRI	HIRI	HARI	GURI	ZURI	ZUEI	HAIEI
NIK		niezazkiakeen / niezazkinakeen	niezazkiokeen		niezazkizukeen	niezazkizuekeen	niezazkiekeen
HIK	hiezazkidakeen		hiezazkiokeen	hiezazkigukeen			hiezazkiekeen
HARK	ziezazkidakeen	ziezazkiakeen / ziezazkinakeen	ziezazkiokeen	ziezazkigukeen	ziezazkizukeen	ziezazkizuekeen	ziezazkiekeen
GUK		geniezazkiakeen/ geniezazkinakeen	geniezazkiokeen		geniezazkizukeen	geniezazkizuekeen	geniezazkiekeen
ZUK	zeniezazkidakeen		zeniezazkiokeen	zeniezazkigukeen			zeniezazkiekeen
ZUEK	zeniezazkidaketen		zeniezazkioketen	zeniezazkiguketen			zeniezazkieketen
HAIEK	ziezazkidaketen	ziezazkiaketen / ziezazkinaketen	ziezazkioketen	ziezazkiguketen	ziezazkizuketen	ziezazkizueketen	ziezazkieketen

ARIKETAK

Esan zeniezazkigukeèn ipuinei ez genieke erantzunik emango

We wouldn't give any response to the stories you could have told us.

Eraman ziezazkiokeèn makinak ez lirateke hemengoak izango

The machines he could have taken him wouldn't be from here.

Eman geniezazkiokeèn egunkariak ez lirateke euskaldunak izango, erdaldunak baizik

The papers we could have given him wouldn't have been in Basque but in a foreign language.

Idatz niezazkiekeèn lanak balio guttikoak izango lirateke

The works I could have written them would be of little value.

Konta ziezazkiguketèn esamesak ez lirateke egiazkoak izango

The rumors they could have told us wouldn't have been true.

ZER - NORI - NORK

4.8.a.- Subjuntibozko orainaldia

Eman diezaiodan = so that I will give it to him.

Eman diezaiodala = (for) me to give it to him.

	NIRI	HIRI	HARI	GURI	ZURI	ZUEI	HAIEI
NIK		diezaadan / diezaanadan	diezaiodan		diezazudan	diezazuedan	diezaiedan
HIK	diezadaan / diezadanan		diezaioan / diezaionan	diezaguan / diezagunan			diezaiean / diezaienan
HARK	diezadan	diezaan / diezanan	diezaion	diezagun	diezazun	diezazuen	diezaien
GUK		diezaagun / diezaanagun	diezaiogun		diezazugun	diezazuegun	diezaiegun
ZUK	diezadazun		diezaiozun	diezaguzun			diezaiezun
ZUEK	diezadazuen		diezaiozuen	diezaguzuen			diezaiezuen
HAIEK	diezadaten	diezaaten / diezanaten	diezaioten	diezaguten	diezazuten	diezazueten	diezaieten

ARIKETAK

Amak esan dit pakete hau eman diezazu-
dala

Mother has told me to give you this package.

Gurasoek esan didate ez diezaiezuela
itxadon

My parents said for you not to wait for them.

Etorri da euritako hori eman diezaiozun

He has come for that umbrella (so that you
will give it to him).

Deitu zaituztegu makina hau konpon die-
zaguzuen

We've called you to fix this machine for us
(so that you will...).

Bat bidaliko dizut, garbigailua konpon
diezazuen

I'll send you a man to fix the washing machine for you.

Dendariak ahaleginak egin ditu, telebista
eros diezaiogun

The salesman has done everything possible to
get us to buy the TV.

Telebista eros diezaiogula eskatu digu

He has asked us to buy the TV from him.

Telefonoz dei diezaiezula esan dit

He said for you to phone them.

Hemen nator, jantzi berri bat egin die-
zadazun

I'm here to get you to make me a new outfit.

Sarrera gisa esan diezazudan...

So that I can tell you this as a sort of intro-
duction...

Banku txeke bat bidaliko diet, arinago
ordain diezazueten

I'll send them a bank check so that they'll pay
you sooner.

Gaia sakon aztertuko dut, entzuleei ondo
azal diezaiedan

I'll examine the subject carefully so that I can
explain it well to the audience.

ZER - NORI - NORK

4.8.b.- Subjuntibozko orainaldia

Eman **diezazkiodan** = so that I will give them to him.

Eman **diezazkiodala** = (for) me to give them to him.

	NIRI	HIRI	HARI	GURI	ZURI	ZUEI	HAIEI
NIK		diezazkiadan / diezazkinadan	diezazkiodan		diezazkizudan	diezazkizuedan	diezazkiedan
HIK	diezazkidaan / diezazkidanan		diezazkioan / diezazkionan	diezazkiguan / diezazkigunan			diezazkiean / diezazkienan
HARK	diezazkidan	diezazkian / diezazkinan	diezazkion	diezazkigun	diezazkizun	diezazkizuen	diezazkien
GUK		diezazkiagun / diezazkinagun	diezazkiogun		diezazkizugun	diezazkizuegun	diezazkiegun
ZUK	diezazkidazun		diezazkiozun	diezazkiguzun			diezazkiezun
ZUEK	diezazkidazuen		diezazkiozuen	diezazkiguzuen			diezazkiezuen
HAIEK	diezazkidaten	diezazkiaten / diezazkinaten	diezazkioten	diezazkiguten	diezazkizuten	diezazkizueten	diezazkieten

ARIKETAK

Amak eskatu dit eraman diezazkiodala kutxa hauk

Mother has asked me to take him these boxes.

Gurasoek semearen fitxak eman diezazkiezuela nahi dute

The parents want you to give them their son's exercises.

Ordaindu egingo diogu, euritakoak eman diezazkigun

We'll pay him to give us the umbrellas.

Makinak ekarri dizkizuegu, konpon diezazkiguzuen

We've brought you the machines so that you can fix them for us.

Langile bat joango zaizue, garbigailuak konpon diezazkizuen

A mechanic will go (to you) to fix the washing machines for you.

Ipin zaitezte hilaran, gozokiak eman diezazkizuegun

Get in line so we can give you the treats.

Idatz ditzagun hitzak argi, irakurleek zuzen uler diezazkiguten

Let's write the words clearly so that the readers will understand us correctly.

Irratiak ekarri dizkizut, konpon diezazkidazun

I've brought you the radios so that you can fix them for me.

ZER - NORI - NORK

4.9.a.- Subjuntibozko lehenaldia

Eman niezaion = so that I would give it to him.
Eman niezaiola = (for) me to give it to him.

	NIRI	HIRI	HARI	GURI	ZURI	ZUEI	HAIEI
NIK		niezaan / niezanan	niezaion		niezazun	niezazuen	niezaien
HIK	hiezadan		hiezaion	hiezagun			hiezaien
HARK	ziezadan (liezadan....)	ziezaan / ziezanan	ziezaion	ziezagun	ziezazun	ziezazuen	ziezaien
GUK		geniezaan / geniezanan	geniezaion		geniezazun	geniezazuen	geniezaien
ZUK	zeniezadan		zeniezaion	zeniezagun			zeniezaien
ZUEK	zeniezadaten		zeniezaioten	zeniezaguten			zeniezaieten
HAIEK	ziezadaten (liezadaten…)	ziezaaten / ziezanaten	ziezaioten	ziezaguten	ziezazuten	ziezazueten	ziezaieten

ARIKETAK

Arretaz lan egin zuen, ongi irten ziezaion

He worked with care so that it would turn out well.

Termometroa eman niezaiola eskatu zidan

He asked me to give him the thermometer.

Ongi gorde zeniezadala eskatu nizun, baina galdu egin didazu

I asked you to keep it safe for me, but you have lost it.

Eman nizun, gorde zeniezadan

I gave it to you to keep for me.

Ezkutatu zuen ikus ez zeniezaien

He hid it so that you wouldn't see it (re: them).

Donibanera bidali genuen, medizina ekar ziezagun

We sent him to San Juan de Luz to bring us the medicine.

Txakur bat erosi genion, excea zain ziezaien

We bought him a dog so that it would guard the house for them.

Txakur bat eros geniezaiela eskatu ziguten

They asked us to buy them a dog.

ZER - NORI - NORK

4.9.b.- Subjuntibozko lehenaldia

Eman niezazkion = so that I would give them to him.
Eman niezazkiola = (for) me to give them to him.

	NIRI	HIRI	HARI	GURI	ZURI	ZUEI	HAIEI
NIK		niezazkian / niezazkinan	niezazkion		niezazkizun	niezazkizuen	niezazkien
HIK	hiezazkidan		hiezazkion	hiezazkigun			hiezazkien
HARK	ziezazkidan (liezazkidan...)	ziezazkian / ziezazkinan	ziezazkion	ziezazkigun	ziezazkizun	ziezazkizuen	ziezazkien
GUK		geniezazkian / geniezazkinan	geniezazkion		geniezazkizun	geniezazkizuen	geniezazkien
ZUK	zeniezazkidan		zeniezazkion	zeniezazkigun			zeniezazkien
ZUEK	zeniezazkidaten		zeniezazkioten	zeniezazkiguten			zeniezazkieten
HAIEK	ziezazkidaten (liezazkidaten...)	ziezázkiaten / ziezazkinaten	ziezazkioten	ziezazkiguten	ziezazkizuten	ziezazkizueten	ziezazkieten

ARIKETAK

Paper haik eman nizkizuen, gorde zenie-
zazkidaten

I gave you those papers so that you would keep them for me.

Paper haik gorde zeniezazkidatela esan nizuen

I told you to keep those papers for me.

Aurrean joan ginen, bizikleta berriak ikus zeniezazkigun

We went in front so you would see our new bicycles.

Soldata handiagoak ordain ziezazkigula es-katu genion nagusiari

We asked the boss to pay us higher salaries.

Nagusiarengana joan ginen, soldata ho-beak ordain ziezazkigun

We went to the boss so that he would pay us better salaries.

ZER - NORI - NORK

4.10.a.- Inperatiboa   Eman biezaio   =   He must give it to him.

	NIRI	HIRI	HARI	GURI	ZURI	ZUEI	HAIEI
NIK							
HIK	iezadak / iezadan		iezaiok / iezaion	iezaguk / iezagun			iezaiek / iezaien
HARK	biezat	biezak / biezan	biezaio	biezagu	biezazu	biezazue	biezaie
GUK							
ZUK	iezadazu		iezaiozu	iezaguzu			iezaiezu
ZUEK	iezadazue		iezaiozue	iezaguzue			iezaiezue
HAIEK	biezadate	biezaate / biezanate	biezaiote	biezagute	biezazute	biezazuete	biezaiete

ARIKETAK

Gorde iezadazu lapitz hau bihar arte
Mesedez esan iezaguzu egia
Ez iezaguzue gezurrik esan
Ordain biezagute zuzentasunez

Keep this pencil for me till tomorrow.
Please tell us the truth.
Don't tell us lies.
They must pay us right.

Eman biezaio berea
Ez iezaiezue minik eman

He must give her what's hers.
Don't hurt them.

Ekar biezaiote mailua
Har iezaiozue zerra
Konpon iezaiozu erlojua
Egin iezadazue txeke hau
Ordain iezaguzue taloia
Lagun iezaiozu Bankura
Eman biezaio zigarroari sua

They must bring him the hammer.
Take the saw from him.
Fix the watch for him.
Write this check for me.
Cash the check for us.
Accompany him to the Bank.
Let him light her cigarette.

Atera iezaiezue afaria

Bring them their dinner.

ZER · NORI · NORK

4.10.b.- Inperatiboa   Eman biezazkio   = He must give them to him.

	NIRI	HIRI	HARI	GURI	ZURI	ZUEI	HAIEI
NIK							
HIK	iezazkidak / iezazkidan		iezazkiok / iezazkion	iezazkiguk / iezazkigun			iezazkiek / iezazkien
HARK	biezazkit	biezazkik / biezazkin	biezazkio	biezazkigu	biezazkizu	biezazkizue	biezazkie
GUK							
ZUK	iezazkidazu		iezazkiozu	iezazkiguzu			iezazkiezu
ZUEK	iezazkidazue		iezazkiozue	iezazkiguzue			iezazkiezue
HAIEK	biezazkidate	biezazkiate / biezazkinate	biezazkiote	biezazkigute	biezazkizute	biezazkizuete	biezazkiete

ARIKETAK

Eros iezazkidazu intzaurrak	Buy me (some) walnuts.
Ekar iezazkiozu poxpoluak	Bring him (some) matches.
Har biezazkio zinemarako txartelak	Buy the movie tickets from him.
Eman iezazkidazue jaialdirako sarrerak	Give me tickets for the festival.
Ez iezazkiezu eraman bizikletak	Don't take them the bikes.
Konpon iezazkiguzue kutxa hauk	Fix these boxes for us.
Bete iezazkiezue edalontziak	Fill their glasses.

DEKLINABIDEA

SINGULARRA

Bizidunak

Bokalez bukatzean

Seme **A**
Seme **AK**
Seme **ARI**
Seme **AREN**
Seme **ARENTZAT**
Seme **ARENGATIK**
Seme **AREKIN**

Seme **AZ**

Seme **ARENGAN**
Seme **ARENGANDIK**
Seme **ARENGANA**
Seme **ARENGANAINO**
Seme **ARENGANANTZ**
Seme **ARENGANAKO**

Kontsonantez

Gizon **A**
Gizon **AK**
Gizon **ARI**
Gizon **AREN**
Gizon **ARENTZAT**
Gizon **ARENGATIK**
Gizon **AREKIN**

Gizon **AZ**

Gizon **ARENGAN**
Gizon **ARENGANDIK**
Gizon **ARENGANA**
Gizon **ARENGANAINO**
Gizon **ARENGANANTZ**
Gizon **ARENGANAKO**

Bizigabeak

Etxe **A**
Etxe **AK**
Etxe **ARI**
Etxe **AREN**
Etxe **ARENTZAT**
Etxe **ARENGATIK**
Etxe **AREKIN**

Etxe **AZ**

Etxe **AN**
Etxe **TIK**
Etxe **RA**
Etxe **RAINO**
Etxe **RANTZ**
Etxe **RAKO**
Etxe **KO**

Gurpil **A**
Gurpil **AK**
Gurpil **ARI**
Gurpil **AREN**
Gurpil **ARENTZAT**
Gurpil **ARENGATIK**
Gurpil **AREKIN**

Gurpil **AZ**

Gurpil-e-**AN**
Gurpil-e-**TIK**
Gurpil-e-**RA**
Gurpil-e-**RAINO**
Gurpil-e-**RANTZ**
Gurpil-e-**RAKO**
Gurpil-e-**KO**

PLURALA

Bizidunak

Bokalez bukatzean

Seme **AK**
Seme **EK**
Seme **EI**
Seme **EN**
Seme **ENTZAT**
Seme **ENGATIK**
Seme **EKIN**

Seme **EZ**

seme **ENGAN**
Seme **ENGANDIK**
Seme **ENGANA**
Seme **ENGANAINO**
Seme **ENGANANTZ**
Seme **ENGANAKO**

—

Kontsonantez

Artzain **AK**
Artzain **EK**
Artzain **EI**
Artzain **EN**
Artzain **ENTZAT**
Artzain **ENGATIK**
Artzain **EKIN**

Artzain **EZ**

Artzain **ENGAN**
Artzain **ENGANDIK**
Artzain **ENGANA**
Artzain **ENGANAINO**
Artzain **ENGANANTZ**
Artzain **ENGANAKO**

—

Bizigabeak

Etxe **AK**
Etxe **EK**
Etxe **EI**
Etxe **EN**
Etxe **ENTZAT**
Etxe **ENGATIK**
Etxe **EKIN**

Etxe **EZ**

Etxe **ETAN**
Etxe **ETATIK**
Etxe **ETARA**
Etxe **ETARAINO**
Etxe **ETARANTZ**
Etxe **ETARAKO**
Etxe **ETAKO**

Zuhaitz **AK**
Zuhaitz **EK**
Zuhaitz **EI**
Zuhaitz **EN**
Zuhaitz **ENTZAT**
Zuhaitz **ENGATIK**
Zuhaitz **EKIN**

Zuhaitz **EZ**

Zuhaitz **ETAN**
Zuhaitz **ETATIK**
Zuhaitz **ETARA**
Zuhaitz **ETARAINO**
Zuhaitz **ETARANTZ**
Zuhaitz **ETARAKO**
Zuhaitz **ETAKO**

MUGAGABEA

Bizidunak

Bokalez bukatzean

Andre
Andre   K
Andre-R-I
Andre-R-EN
Andre-R-ENTZAT
Andre-R-ENGATIK
Andre-R-EKIN

Andre   Z

—
—
—
—
—
—
—

Kontsonantez

Jaun
Jaun-E-K
Jaun   I
Jaun   EN
Jaun   ENTZAT
Jaun   ENGATIK
Jaun   EKIN

Jaun-E-Z

—
—
—
—
—
—
—

Bizigabeak

Mendi
Mendi   K
Mendi-R-I
Mendi-R-EN
Mendi-R-ENTZAT
Mendi-R-ENGATIK
Mendi-R-EKIN

Mendi   Z

Mendi   TAN
Mendi   TATIK
Mendi   TARA
Mendi   TARAINO
Mendi   TARANTZ
Mendi   TARAKO
Mendi   TAKO

Oihan
Oihan-E-K
Oihan   I
Oihan   EN
Oihan   ENTZAT
Oihan   ENGATIK
Oihan   EKIN

Oihan-E-Z

Oihan-E-TAN
Oihan-E-TATIK
Oihan-E-TARA
Oihan-E-TARAINO
Oihan-E-TARANTZ
Oihan-E-TARAKO
Oihan-E-TAKO

PLURAL HURBILA

Bizidunak

Bokalez bukatzean	Kontsonantez
Emakume **OK**	Giputz **OK**
Emakume **OK**	Giputz **OK**
Emakume **OI**	Giputz **OI**
Emakume **ON**	Giputz **ON**
Emakume **ONTZAT**	Giputz **ONTZAT**
Emakume **ONGATIK**	Giputz **ONGATIK**
Emakume **OKIN**	Giputz **OKIN**
Emakume **OZ**	Giputz **OZ**
Emakume **ONGAN**	Giputz **ONGAN**
Emakume **ONGANDIK**	Giputz **ONGANDIK**
Emakume **ONGANA**	Giputz **ONGANA**
Emakume **ONGANAINO**	Giputz **ONGANAINO**
Emakume **ONGANANTZ**	Giputz **ONGANANTZ**
Emakume **ONGANAKO**	Giputz **ONGANAKO**
—	—

Bizigabeak

Lege **OK**	Haran **OK**
Lege **OK**	Haran **OK**
Lege **OI**	Haran **OI**
Lege **ON**	haran **ON**
Lege **ONTZAT**	Haran **ONTZAT**
Lege **ONGATIK**	Haran **ONGATIK**
Lege **OKIN**	Haran **OKIN**
Lege **OZ**	Haran **OZ**
Lege **OTAN**	Haran **OTAN**
Lege **OTATIK**	Haran **OTATIK**
Lege **OTARA**	Haran **OTARA**
Lege **OTARAINO**	Haran **OTARAINO**
Lege **OTARANTZ**	Haran **OTARANTZ**
Lege **OTARAKO**	Haran **OTARAKO**
Lege **OTAKO**	Haran **OTAKO**

ERAKUSLEEN DEKLINABIDEA

HAU	HORI	HURA	HAUK	HORIK	HAIK
HON-e-K	HORR-e-K	HAR K	HAU EK	HORI EK	HAI EK
HON I	HORR I	HAR I	HAU EI	HORI EI	HAI EI
HON EN	HORR EN	HAR EN	HAU EN	HORI EN	HAI EN
HON ENTZAT	HORR ENTZAT	HAR ENTZAT	HAU ENTZAT	HORI ENTZAT	HAI ENTZAT
HON EGATIK	HORR EGATIK	HAR GATIK	HAU ENGATIK	HORI ENGATIK	HAI ENGATIK
HON EKIN	HORR EKIN	HAR EKIN	HAU EKIN	HORI EKIN	HAI EKIN
HON-e-TAZ	HORR-e-TAZ	HAR TAZ	HAU ETAZ	HORI ETAZ	HAI ETAZ
HON ENGAN	HORR ENGAN	HAR ENGAN	HAU ENGAN	HORI ENGAN	HAI ENGAN
HON ENGANDIK	HORR ENGANDIK	HAR ENGANDIK	HAU ENGANDIK	HORI ENGANDIK	HAI ENGANDIK
HON ENGANA	HORR ENGANA	HAR ENGANA	HAU ENGANA	HORI ENGANA	HAI ENGANA
HON ENGANAINO	HORR ENGANAINO	HAR ENGANAINO	HAU ENGANAINO	HORI ENGANAINO	HAI ENGANAINO
HON ENGANANTZ	HORR ENGANANTZ	HAR ENGANANTZ	HAU ENGANANTZ	HORI ENGANANTZ	HAI ENGANANTZ
HON ENGANAKO	HORR ENGANAKO	HAR ENGANAKO	HAU ENGANAKO	HORI ENGANAKO	HAI ENGANAKO
HON ETAN	HORR ETAN	HAR TAN	HAU ETAN	HORI ETAN	HAI ETAN
HON ETATIK	HORR ETATIK	HAR TATIK	HAU ETATIK	HORI ETATIK	HAI ETATIK
HON ETARA	HORR ETARA	HAR TARA	HAU ETARA	HORI ETARA	HAI ETARA
HON ETARAINO	HORR ETARAINO	HAR TARAINO	HAU ETARAINO	HORI ETARAINO	HAI ETARAINO
HON ETARANTZ	HORR ETARANTZ	HAR TARANTZ	HAU ETARANTZ	HORI ETARANTZ	HAI ETARANTZ
HON ETARAKO	HORR ETARAKO	HAR TARAKO	HAU ETARAKO	HORI ETARAKO	HAI ETARAKO
HON ETAKO	HORR ETAKO	HAR TAKO	HAU ETAKO	HORI ETAKO	HAI ETAKO

IZENORDE PERTSONALEN DEKLINABIDEA

(Ni, hi, gu, zu, zuek)

NI	HI	GU	ZU	ZUEK
NIK	HIK	GUK	ZUK	ZUEK
NIRI	HIRI	GURI	ZURI	ZUEI
ENE	HIRE	GURE	ZURE	ZUEN
NIreTZAT	HIreTZAT	GUreTZAT	ZUreTZAT	ZUENTZAT
NIreGATIK	HIreGATIK	GUreGATIK	ZUreGATIK	ZUENGATIK
NIreKIN	HIreKIN	GUreKIN	ZUreKIN	ZUEKIN
NITAZ	HITAZ	GUTAZ	ZUTAZ	ZUETAZ
NIreGAN	HIreGAN	GUreGAN	ZUreGAN	ZUENGAN
NIreGANDIK	HIreGANDIK	GUreGANDIK	ZUreGANDIK	ZUENGANDIK
NIreGANA	HIreGANA	GUreGANA	ZUreGANA	ZUENGANA
NIreGANAINO	HIreGANAINO	GUreGANAINO	ZUreGANAINO	ZUENGANAINO
NIreGANANTZ	HIreGANANTZ	GUreGANANTZ	ZUreGANANTZ	ZUENGANANTZ
NIreGANAKO	HIreGANAKO	GUreGANAKO	ZUreGANAKO	ZUENGANAKO
—	—	—	—	—

OHARRA. — Hirugarren pertsonetan aurreko horrialdeko erakus-
leak erabiltzen dira askotan.

Printed in the United States
134772LV00003B/10/P